ARON
ABRAHAMSEN:

ON WINGS
OF SPIRIT

ARON ABRAHAMSEN:

ON WINGS OF SPIRIT

BY ARON ABRAHAMSEN
WITH
DORIS ABRAHAMSEN
AND
DON MAGARY

A.R.E. Press
Sixty-Eighth & Atlantic Avenue
P.O. Box 656
Virginia Beach, VA 23451-0656

Library of Congress Cataloging-in-Publication Data

Abrahamsen, Aron, 1921-

Aron Abrahamsen: on wings of spirit / by Aron Abrahamsen; with Doris Abrahamsen and Don Magary.

p.   cm.

ISBN 0-87604-298-1

1. Abrahamsen, Aron, 1921- . 2. Psychics—United States—Biography.   3. Converts from Judaism—United States—Biography.   I. Abrahamsen, Doris.   II. Magary, Don.
III. Title.   IV. Title: On wings of spirit.

BF1027.A27A3   1993

133.8'092--dc20

[B]   92-42662
                                                            CIP

Dedicated to
Diane and Dan Lumsden

Acknowledgments

I wish to thank my editor, Dr. Mark Thurston, who with great professional skill, insight, and much patience edited the manuscript and offered many helpful suggestions. Many thanks to Drs. Harmon and June Bro for their suggestions and encouragements. I sincerely appreciate Harmon's helpful corrections and long-enduring patience in reading the manuscript. To Dr. Maria DeRungs-McKinney for supplying the case histories from her research. To Don Magary for his generous offer to help us in the writing of this book, for his invaluable suggestions as to format, and for his professional insight in the presentation of the material. To Rebecca Clark, Marie and David Adams for their encouragement during the writing of this book. I thank friends and family for their respected opinions and encouragements in the assessment of this work. Also, I want to thank those recipients of our readings from which examples were taken to illustrate our work. And loving, loving thanks to my wife Doris who labored so faithfully with me in the preparation of the manuscript. Without her this book could not have been written.

TABLE OF CONTENTS

FOREWORD

As we head into the 21st century, few adventures offer as great a challenge as what this book is about: the process that university researchers call "psi" and familiar discourse calls "psychic" or "intuitive."

In this highly readable autobiographical account, we follow the development of a gift of unusual perception and judgment that has made Aron Abrahamsen, for many years a skilled aerospace engineer, into one of the few most respected practitioners of intuitive counsel in the United States and Japan. Thousands of individuals have turned to him for their personal journeys of discovery in self-understanding and vocational potency, found in the "readings" which he undertakes in a deep meditative state.

Unlike many who claim to "channel" a being from another realm or time, Abrahamsen speaks only of what he directly sees or surmises when in a quietly inspired state that is congruent with his deeply felt prayer life and his biblically oriented faith. In this respect he provides parallels to the efforts of Edgar Cayce, the modern portrait photographer and dedicated churchman who became an astonishing seer in an age that has no place for seers. I listened to hundreds of Cayce's discourses before examining their significance in my graduate degree program at Harvard University and then wrote my doctoral dissertation on Cayce at the University of Chicago. It led me to formulate a set of criteria for evaluating the accuracy, scope, richness of perspective, and dialogical engagement in such counsel. Abrahamsen's work meets these criteria in a way that has held my serious attention for more than twenty years.

I first met Aron through my psychotherapy clients! Having conducted for decades, alongside my teaching, a Jungian practice in hospital and private office settings, I had often been presented with a transcript or a tape in which some astrologer, medium, psychometrist, or other type of intuitive counselor aspired to analyze my client and recommend action. Frankly, I was jaded, and winced whenever a client handed me such material. But when I picked up Aron's typed reading for an attorney I had engaged for months in weekly therapy sessions, I was startled and immediately interested. Here was a portrait that fit, though Aron had never met the man!

In the years that followed, I studied many examples of Aron's work, finding it sensitive, rich, and productive, especially in the opening analytical portion, easier in itself to verify and use than his past-life material. His work for members of my family proved as penetrating as his counsel to my clients, colleagues, and researchers.

Not surprisingly, when I moved to Aron's home area in the Pacific Northwest for five years, I sought him out for long discussions on the content and method of his art. When we could, we met weekly and tape-recorded some of our explorations, drawing also on the clear, orderly mind of his wife Doris. My wife June, who holds a doctorate in religion and Jungian psychology, found as I did that Aron's deep and informed grounding in biblical faith brought him closer to the spirit of Cayce's work, which we had both observed, than to the productions of scores of other psychics we had studied over the years, including Eileen Garrett, Olga Worrall, Arthur Ford, and the Dutchman, Peter Hurkos. It was especially fruitful for us to interview some of the many Japanese who came across the Pacific to meet Aron and get his aid.

To be sure, much research remains to be done on the unusual material reported in this book: patterns of reincarnation and karma, securing one's own intuitive guidance, uncovering ancient buried artifacts, using color and music in healing, sharing in the start of a new era in history, and more. In this book, as in real life, Abrahamsen proves to be self-critical, balanced, humorous, and unpretentious—not wanting to be anyone's guru, but simply sharing his experiences in an obviously disciplined yet pioneering life.

Despite the impressive findings of nearly a century of patient inquiry, going back to William James and before, we still have no adequate theory of "psi" to join together hard-won discoveries into a coherent model that links it to better-known processes of mind, body, and spirit. My own hope, of course, is that Abrahamsen's work, reported so engagingly in this story of a Norwegian immigrant lad growing up to be a sophisticated expert in space technology and then an astronaut in inner space, will catch the interest of some able graduate students ready to do research—such as those I have taught for many years at Harvard, Syracuse, and elsewhere. But just as rewarding would be having thoughtful lay readers find here clues to the safe and helpful development of their own abilities to secure guidance, not as professional psychics but as persons seeking to be more fully alive. For the frontier here is not simply one of mastering handy or colorful unknowns. It is the more compelling frontier of becoming "friends of God," as co-creators of a better world. Crossing that frontier is an adventure not simply for researchers but for all of us.

Harmon Hartzell Bro, Ph.D., Co-Director
Pilgrim Institute
Centerville, Massachusetts

PREFACE

A s I look back, it's almost as if the opportunity to meet and work with Aron Abrahamsen was predestined.

Like any serious student of the paranormal, I was familiar with the psychic work of Aron and his wife Doris. My first recollection of their accomplishments was in 1979 while reading Jeff Goodman's book, *We Are the Earthquake Generation* and later, *Psychic Archaeology*. Goodman had noted that Abrahamsen lived in Oregon, but that was vague so I forgot about it for a while.

Years later, while living in California, I saw Aron's name again and was reminded that I wanted to meet him. The Association for Research and Enlightenment (A.R.E.) was holding a seminar entitled "Be Your Own Psychic" in Anaheim, California. Aron and Doris Abrahamsen were among the featured speakers. Since I travel in my business a great deal, I wasn't sure I would be in town during the seminar, so I procrastinated about registering. When I saw I'd be able to attend, I called the A.R.E. to preregister, but it was too late. The space available was sold out. What a disappointment!

Two days before the meeting, I called again. Almost

pleading, I asked if there was any chance they could work me in. Thankfully there had just been a cancellation, so I made my reservation.

During this period I had made another decision. As a professional writer and magazine editor, I decided that I wanted to give something back. I was looking for a writing project in which I could donate whatever talents I had in some type of service. So I decided to talk to someone from the A.R.E.

During that daylong seminar, I had an opportunity to speak to A.R.E.'s president, Charles Thomas Cayce, about a proposed writing project. Charles Thomas suggested I send him some work samples. Also, during one of the breaks in the seminar, I was able to speak momentarily with Aron and Doris, although just one of a group that had gathered to ask questions.

A couple of months later, after having sent the work samples to Charles Thomas, I followed up by planning a trip to Virginia Beach, Virginia. Charles Thomas referred me to Bob Smith, editor of A.R.E's magazine, *Venture Inward*. During my discussions with Smith, he mentioned that Aron and Doris were collaborating on a book about Aron's life, but they hadn't completed it. He suggested I might want to talk to them.

When I returned home, I called and talked to Doris, explaining that I was searching for a service-related opportunity and that A.R.E. had suggested they might need some help with their book. She was pleasant enough but asked me a lot of questions regarding my spiritual beliefs, religious preferences, and philosophies relating to psychic phenomenon. After we talked for a while, I suggested that I should fly up to Everett, Washington, where they now lived, to meet them. Then we could discuss the project further. They accepted.

During our dinner meeting, I was impressed with

their perspective on their work. It is more than giving psychic readings; it is based on a deep spiritual commitment and their personal search for God. I also noted that Aron has a delightful sense of humor. He takes his work very seriously, but he doesn't take himself too seriously—a human quality I find important.

When we parted that evening, both the Abrahamsens and I pledged to give the project more thought and pray about it. In the meantime, they were to send me a couple of chapters to review. It wasn't too long before I knew that this was the project I had wanted to do and hoped the Abrahamsens felt the same.

When they agreed that I should team up with them, it was as if a dream had come true. For the next year, we worked together, and I made several trips to Everett. I learned that this devoted couple was genuine and sincere. They both looked on their work as a ministry, an opportunity to use Aron's special gift to help others. I entered the project with a deep curiosity about this undertaking and a long list of questions. For example, how does an electrical engineer, of Norwegian heritage, laboring in the aerospace field, end up as a psychic in Washington? How has he reconciled in his mind such an unusual phenomenon and its place in a materialistic-oriented world?

What are some of the ways that he uses his gift? What are some specific examples of the type of information that he brought back and how did it help, change, or increase the value of someone's life?

Aron claims that his gift is nothing that special and that anyone can do it through spiritual focusing. If that's so, why haven't more people achieved it?

I learned that Aron is a man who can see things others cannot. He can see artifacts buried thousands of years beneath tons of earth, a phenomenon that baffles scientific minds and defies normal, reasonable thinking. Yet he isn't sitting at the right hand of political power brokers, advising them of astute maneuvers; nor is he making and breaking corporate financiers in the game of fortunes. He strolls peaceably, almost unnoticed, along the banks of Puget Sound, a humble man, a man who loves and serves God, making his remarkable gift available to anyone.

How does he do this? What secrets does he know? What are the limits of his power? He simply sits down in his favorite chair, closes his eyes, prays, and listens meditatively to God. Then, miraculously, he is taken on an astral journey to the Akashic records, the most remarkable library known to the human mind. It's a place where ideas of eternal life, reincarnation, and karma aren't philosophical theories, but concrete universal concepts etched forever on the skein of time and space.

This humble man of God, a prophet in modern times, through the aid of spiritual guides can request anyone's record and read these timeless manuscripts, determining and interpreting the karmic purposes of a soul's current life.

So this, then, is the remarkable story of Aron Abrahamsen and his wife Doris. It's the story of the Abrahamsens' personal quest for spiritual development. It answers questions. It probes the mysteries of life.

Don Magary
Tempe, Arizona
October, 1992

When we walk to the edge of all the light we have,

and take the step into the darkness of the unknown,

we must believe one of two things will happen:

There will be something solid

for us to stand on,

or we will be taught how to fly.

Claire Norris

CHAPTER ONE
INTO THE UNKNOWN

Alone on deck, I waved goodbye into the darkness. Though I couldn't see them, I knew Mother and my older brother, Heiman, were on the dock—no doubt waving to me. Mother was sending me to New York with all the family valuables for safekeeping until the volatile conditions in Europe ended—and who knew how long that would be!

It was 10 p.m., January 24, 1940.

The SS *Bergensfjord* left Oslo, Norway, on its regularly scheduled voyage to the United States. Tense political conditions and the impending threat of war had forced the Norwegian government to declare a total blackout. No lights were visible on the pier nor on the ship.

Eighteen years old, traveling alone and scared. Thankfully, I had been assured that Sam, one of my other brothers, would join me in Bergen and that helped calm me some. But as I learned early in my journey to an unknown land, even the best-laid plans don't always work out. As it turned out, a whole new life filled with challenges was ahead.

I glanced around the empty deck. Other passengers hadn't even bothered to wave goodbye. What was the use? They couldn't see anyone either. They had wisely escaped from the cold, damp air to the warmth and security of their staterooms. Everybody except me. I squinted into the night, hoping to catch one last glimpse of Mother and Heiman behind on the pier. All I saw was blackness.

Slowly, cautiously, under the protection of darkness, the giant steamer cast its mooring lines and slipped silently through the Oslofjord.

Finally, I made my way to my cabin. I was more alone than I had ever been in my life, and a feeling of isolation and sadness engulfed me. But the importance of this trip gave me courage—my family was depending on me to take the trunks of silver household items to America where they would be safe. I knew that these trunks, sealed and locked, were safe for now, stowed far below in the hold of the ship.

My thoughts wandered back to three days earlier when we arrived in Oslo by train from my hometown, Trondheim. It took until the day of my departure to secure all the documents needed for my mission to America.

That same evening at 9 p.m., we left the Grand Hotel, where we had stayed, for the ship. As I sat in the taxi, between my mother and brother, I wondered what the future held for me. Shortly, I would be away from my family. Away from the warmth, care, and security I had known all my life. What would happen to me? Could I take care of myself?

The trip to the pier was short. We arrived sooner than I wanted to and the big ship waited. I became very nervous.

I bid goodbye to my brother and kissed Mother. Tears of concern rolled down her face. Our lips met as we said "Shalom." I can still hear her say "Goodbye, my child . . . take care of yourself. Stay well."

Two days later the ship arrived in Bergen, where my brother Sam was to join me and we would travel to America together. A telegram delivered to me told a different story: "Sam not able to travel with you. Stop. Don't cancel your trip. Stop. Continue on to America. Stop. Love, Mother. Stop."

I was devastated!

Me, traveling alone to that far country, America? I knew so little English. I wasn't sure I could get along. Bewildered, confused, and terrified, I went back to my small cabin, which suddenly seemed spacious now that Sam wouldn't be sharing it with me. It would be a lonely journey. My thoughts immediately shot to the trunks in the hold. A sensation of panic rushed through me. Should I take the trunks and all my belongings off the ship and return to Trondheim? Frantically I searched for a phone and was directed to one on the pier.

I rushed as fast as I could and was able to get a line to Trondheim. My mother answered, and I told her what my plans were—to return home. But she insisted that I go to America. "By all means, don't come home. You must find the courage to continue your travel. Goodbye, my son, and . . ." The connection was broken. The phone line was needed for a high-priority call, I was told by the operator. The ship was about to leave, and again I ran back before it was too late.

On the promenade deck, bathed in sunlight, the crew made the ship ready through a flurry of shouted commands. "Cast off starboard bow line! Let go the aft lines! Secure all lines! Slow ahead."

On the pier far below the deck from where I watched, people waved and shouted their goodbyes to friends and loved ones. Among that sea of bodies beaming their emotions to their departing family and friends, there was not one familiar face nor one smile cast toward me. Nobody waved goodbye to me. Feeling even more empty, more alone, I said goodbye under my breath to my native country on that cold winter day. It was January 26, 1940.

En route, I mingled with the other passengers but was too shy to initiate a conversation. I didn't know what to say, so I kept to myself most of the time. Once I listened to a lively interchange among several passengers. One said, "America? Nobody helps anybody in America. From the moment you arrive in New York, you're on your own. America is a tough, hard country. Everybody is busy caring for their own needs. They'll have no time to help any of us. You simply must help yourself."

Swallowing hard, trying to clear the lump in my throat, I realized this adventure that had been thrust upon me was going to be even rougher than I had visualized. Panic set in, and I wanted to jump in the ocean and swim home. What was I to do? To whom could I turn for advice and comfort? My prospects for the immediate future didn't look very promising.

That evening I went to sleep with these depressing thoughts racing through my consciousness and awakened hoping the night would have provided peace and answers. It hadn't. Outside, an Atlantic winter storm was raging very much like the tempest roaring inside me—discouragement, great fear, misgivings, and doubts.

Days passed, and the ship drew ever closer to New York. If I had my wish, the ship would never dock, so I wouldn't have to face New York alone. My mind echoed with that dreadful threat: "In America, no one will help you; you're on your own; you'll have to help yourself." I had never before been on my own. I experienced fear such as I had never suffered before.

On Saturday, February 3, the SS *Bergensfjord* tied up to its assigned berth on the Hudson River. Passengers called to relatives, friends, and loved ones waiting on the pier. I noticed how happy they seemed. Not me.

After the usual ceremonies following a ship's arrival in a foreign port, passengers were permitted to leave. I watched as friends and relatives greeted each other with tears of laughter and joy followed by compassionate hugs. No one welcomed or hugged me.

I was among the last to disembark. Having secured a student visa valid for only three months from the immigration officers who had taken positions on board ship, I took a deep breath and stepped into America.

When I reached the dock, my sealed and locked trunks were waiting—along with the U.S. Customs officers. My inability to speak or understand very much English brought me into immediate conflict. Through their gestures and attitude, I learned that the customs officials wanted to know what was inside my trunks. I tried to communicate in my broken English that it was our family's treasures which I had brought to America for safekeeping, but my lack of skill to make it clear led them to believe that it was items I had brought to sell. After several frustrating minutes, the officers handed me a receipt and took my trunks into custody.

Now, not only afraid and intimidated, I felt as if I were a failure at the task I had been given—to protect the family fortune until my brother Sam could come to help me find a place to store the trunks where they would be safe. I watched as the trunks were taken away, wondering if I would ever see them again.

Before disembarking, a lady passenger had asked me where I planned to stay. I told her that I didn't know. Her husband suggested the YMCA on 34th Street where I could stay for 75 cents a night. She scribbled the address on a small piece of paper and slipped it into my hand. I approached a taxi and handed the paper to the taxi driver. He nodded his head yes and motioned for me to get in.

New York was more than I expected. I was awestruck by the noise, the towering buildings, and the general fast-paced activities of its inhabitants. I had never seen a city like this before. I felt very small compared to the immenseness of all this.

At the YMCA I rented a room. Well, it wasn't much of a room. If I'd have walked in too fast, I'd have fallen right out of the window. But for a while, at least, this would be my home. A far cry—and cry I did—from my home in Norway. I was homesick, but had to push those emotions aside because I had things to do and no idea how I was going to accomplish them.

"No one will help you; you are on your own; you will have to help yourself." This was my reality. I remembered these words as I sat alone on the only chair—a hard wooden one—in my room wondering what to do. It was obvious I needed to do something. But what?

The first thing that came to mind was to locate a distant relative. Before I had left Trondheim, my sister who was visiting from Amsterdam had given me the name of her husband's sister who lived in New York. I was about to come face to face with the perils of finding my way around New York City. I summoned up my courage and started toward the lobby.

As I approached the desk clerk, I noticed an alarming sign on my left, "Help yourself." That's terrible, I thought. Americans are even advertising that they aren't going to help me. Later, I realized that some free material was being offered, and this was the American way of saying "take all you need."

I handed the clerk the piece of paper my sister had given with the address, and I asked in my best English "Vere is this address?" He studied it for a while, looked at a map, and came back with the following information: "Walk over to Broadway, turn right, walk two blocks, take the subway to 96th Street, and you are there."

This would have been fine except for a few minor details. I didn't know what a "block" was, had no idea where Broadway was, had never seen a subway and wouldn't know one if it fell on me. "Vat is a block?" I asked. The clerk drew a little map, marking with an "X" the YMCA's location. Then he drew an arrow from the YMCA toward another street, which he marked "Broadway." With great patience and in precise detail, he explained what a block was. He drew two squares on the paper, separated from each other by a little space. Pointing to one square he said, "This is one block and this is another block," as he pointed to the second square. I understood.

"After you have walked two blocks, cross the street. On the corner there is a stairway going down. Walk down this stairway, put a nickel in the turnstile and walk through it. Go to the right side of the platform. Take the first subway. Get off at the next stop. That's 96th Street. Walk upstairs to the street level, turn left, the address is in the middle of the block on the right side." Between interruptions and more explanations, such as "nickel" and "turnstile," I finally got the whole message.

I gave him a well-rehearsed "Thank you" and "Very vell" and was on my way. I appreciated his not making fun of me and sincerely trying to help me.

I walked toward Broadway, quite happy that I had

come this far without getting lost; turned right and counted, very carefully, two blocks and two street crossings. After the second street crossing, much to my delight, right in front of me was the stairway leading down to the subway. I was relieved that I was finding my way around.

Before I went downstairs, I looked around to note a few landmarks so that I would recognize the area when I returned. Several movie houses on the block were all lit up, so I thought they would be good landmarks. Across the street there were a few stores but no movie houses.

I found the turnstile, dropped a nickel in the slot, and walked to the right side of the platform. A train arrived at high speed, stopped abruptly, and like magic all the entrance doors flew open. People rushed out like ants. I boarded and found a seat just as the train started to move. The train was stuffy and filthy.

At the first stop I got off, found the stairway, walked up to the street level, and there it was—96th Street. The address was just where the clerk at the YMCA said it would be. Thanks to a helpful American desk clerk and his kindness, I was able to spend my first evening in New York getting acquainted with relatives I had never met before.

I found my new relatives to be lovely people, very kind and patient with my attempts to speak English. We tried to talk about family and the dangerous situation in Europe. That was the subject which lay heavily on our minds.

It was now approaching 10 p.m., and I thought it best to leave and go back to my room at the YMCA. My relatives suggested I wait a few minutes until after they had listened to the news report. On the radio an English-speaking voice spoke loudly and rapidly. Then several trumpets sounded a fanfare, some more rapid talking, a few more fanfares, and then all was quiet for a few moments. Finally it started! A very swift voice going at lightning speed, like a machine gun, began shooting out word after word. The voice was one which demanded attention, and it kept talking like water coming full force out of a spigot. There was no stopping, but a continual downpour of words and phrases. Then, as suddenly as it started, the voice stopped. More fanfares, the loud voice came on again, a few more fanfares. Then silence. Finally the radio was turned off, and I was told, "The news is over."

But while the newscast was on, it sounded to me like an auction—I didn't understand one word. I wanted to know about the situation in Europe. Were the Germans still advancing? How was the war between Russia and Finland going? What were the United States and England doing? I was very frustrated. Though my relatives did their best to explain to me what was going on, I just nodded my head. I didn't understand what they were trying to say either and was too embarrassed to admit it.

The newscast was my first introduction to the "Richfield Reporter," heard every night from 10 to 10:15, and one which I later listened to every evening. It was now 10:30 and I wanted to get back to my hotel. I was tired. It had been a long day, and I had witnessed many new and strange things: a new city, a new country, a new and different kind of people, a new language, new customs—everything new. But if I thought I had seen it all, there was more coming. It was sneaking up on me, silently, on tiptoes, like a little boy stealing his way into Mother's cookie jar.

As I was leaving, my relatives asked where I was staying—the name of the place, street address, and how I would get there.

I was stunned. For the first time, I realized I had neglected to make a note of the address of the hotel where I was staying. My only record was the slip of paper given to me by the couple aboard ship—and I had given that to the taxi driver.

"I don't know the name of the place nor the address," I admitted. "But I do know how to get there." "How is that?" they asked.

"Simple. I take the subway downtown for one stop, get off, walk upstairs, walk two blocks, turn left, walk one more block, and there I am."

They stood there with their mouths hanging open and suddenly ran for their coats and hats, insisting that they take me to the hotel. I protested, assuring them there was no need for concern.

They took me by the hand and together we walked to the subway.

I didn't realize until some time later that I had taken an express train going up to 96th Street, but we had caught a local train going downtown.

It was 2 a.m. before we finally found my hotel, the Sloane House YMCA. I knew that neither my mother nor any of my eight brothers or two sisters would be waiting in my room when I got there. Being accustomed to having a large family around me, an empty room is very empty. But it was a place to sleep. It was clean, warm, and quiet. I was grateful for it.

My first day in this new country had been quite an experience, filled with the joy of meeting distant relatives and discovering how helpful Americans can be, easing my burden and fear that "No one will help you." It had been also a day of wonderment and adventure, seeing this magnificent city with all its immenseness and thousands of busy people. And it had been a day of disappointment and loneliness. I wondered where my trunks were tonight. I thought of my mother and family so far away. It had only been a few days since I had seen them, but miles and time were exaggerated by my isolation.

As I snuggled my weary head into my pillow that night, my thoughts and dreams were of home and loved ones.

CHAPTER TWO
NEW YORK, NEW YORK

New York is quite a city in the eyes of a boy from Norway. Slowly, the city unveils its mysterious facets, revealing its many moods. In the winter a cold and penetrating wind jumps out of the East River, marches down 42nd Street, turning into a jog and then a sprint across the city. But it doesn't discourage the passersby. These hardy New Yorkers have grown accustomed to its chilling dance and usually pay it little attention. The wind rolls on, whistling a lively tune as it sails across West End Avenue, until finally with a roaring laughter it dives into the Hudson River. This is one of the many faces of New York I remember.

My second day in America was Sunday. I slept late, and by early afternoon I was hungry. I asked the desk clerk where I could eat, and he pointed to a restaurant next door. I walked in and encountered another revelation, another obstacle. There were no tables—only a long counter with chairs that swiveled. I had never seen anything like that before. In Norway, restaurants had tables covered with white linen cloth. Waitresses, dressed in proper uniforms, served whatever you ordered in a courteous and well-behaved manner.

I sat down and the waitress handed me a menu. I opened it and was totally confused. I had no idea what to order. The only thing I understood from the menu was the price for each meal. I studied it for a long while as if it were a treasure map. As soon as I looked up, the waitress approached. She asked what I wanted. All I could do was point to something on the menu. I didn't know what it was nor could I pronounce it. "Ah, chicken croquettes," she said, writing it down on a little pad of paper.

While waiting to be served, I examined the restaurant as best I could. This was a funny-looking place, I thought. Here I sat in a revolving chair next to a long counter. What kind of a restaurant was this? Evidently the Americans had no idea what a real restaurant was like; otherwise, they wouldn't have allowed such peculiar arrangements. This was a brand-new experience for me. Everything was so informal. There was no atmosphere, no dinner music, lots of noise, and people sitting so close together it made me uncomfortable. America certainly was a strange country.

"Pass the salt, will ya?" the fellow next to me asked. That was very rude. Why should I pass the salt? This fellow was a complete stranger to me. He hadn't even introduced himself. This behavior would never have taken place in Norway. I would have to get used to the ways of Americans! I handed him the salt. He didn't even show me the courtesy of saying "thank you."

The waitress came back and asked, "Would you like French or Thousand Island dressing?" What had she said? From her tone of voice I assumed that I was being given a choice, although I didn't understand her words. Contemplating for a moment whether to say yes or no, I replied with a very positive "Yes." She repeated her question and, realizing that I didn't understand, walked away. Shortly she was back with the salad. An orange "sauce" was poured over it. To me it looked like paint. No sooner had I started to eat it than she came back with another plate. It was my dinner. So that's chicken croquettes! It didn't taste too bad. But I wondered why such a dignified name was given to a few cakes of chopped chicken. I supposed that some things would have to have a dignified name to attract attention. The fancier the name and the more difficult to pronounce, the better people would like it. I was learning about the customs of this city, strange as they seemed to me.

On another occasion while I strolled along Broadway, rain started to pour down. I decided that this was a good time to have lunch and ducked into a place called Horn & Hardart, an automat cafeteria. The food was behind glass doors and would open when the correct change was dropped into the appropriate slot. It was easy to order. I could see the food before I bought it, so it wasn't necessary to know what to call it.

I picked up what I wanted and found a table. This place had tables but no linen tablecloths.

While eating, I looked around the place and noticed an old man sitting alone. Maybe he had come in from the rain and was waiting for it to stop so he could continue on his walk. But when the rain stopped, he was still sitting there. I wondered why. He had eaten nothing so far. Then I witnessed one of the kindest acts I had ever seen.

A young, well-dressed lady got up from her table, walked over to the old man and gave him a quarter. I heard him say, "Thank you." As he walked over to the automat to get a sandwich and a cup of coffee, I got a good look at him. He was in his mid-fifties, balding, and he had a drawn, unshaven face. His clothes, two sizes too large, hung on him. He must have been very hungry for he gulped down the sandwich.

The young lady had been sensitive to the needs of the old man and had offered him a coin with which he could buy a little food. America, I discovered, was a generous country. I had never seen this done in Norway. The compassion of the American people was one of the faces I never expected to see in New York.

Another face of New York which remains with me even today was my visits to the New York Library. It was an overwhelming experience for me. In Trondheim there was only one small library with a very limited selection of books. So when I entered the one in New York, it was as if all the personages from ancient history were waiting to teach me. Here Hannibal was still the leader of his battalion of elephants and the strategist of his army's battles; Socrates, Aristotle, and Plato were still concerned about the reality of life; Alexander the Great was still weeping because there were no more empires to conquer. From the depths of those books government leaders, scientists, inventors, rulers, presidents, and commoners were all eager to share with me the benefit of their knowledge and wisdom.

Never before had I seen so many volumes assembled in one area—not only in English, but in many other languages as well. I acquainted myself with this tremendous storehouse of knowledge and started to wonder how I could possibly have time to read all the books available. I spent many hours in this place.

I also became aware of how easy it was to obtain an education in this country. Here, schooling was free up to the college level. It was so much different than my native country. In Norway, the first seven years in the public schools were free, but beyond that it became a different story. Above the primary grades, one was required to pay tuition for middle school and have a bet-ter-than-average grade in order to enter. In addition students paid for books, supplies, and whatever else was needed. After middle school came gymnasium and then university. Years before, my grades from the primary school had been only average; therefore, I had known that I wouldn't be allowed to enter middle school. I was so ashamed of my performance in school that I had cried over my inferior standing.

When the time of my graduation had come near in June 1935, I went before the principal and told him I would be on vacation in the country at the time of the ceremonies. Therefore, I wouldn't be able to attend the exercises. Of course, I wasn't telling the truth. I asked if it would it be possible to have my transcript early. My reason was that at the graduation, as the diplomas were given out, it was the practice at that time to call out, for the whole audience to hear (including all the classmates), the student's name and the overall grade he or she received. What's more, the grade for every course and the overall rating were written on the diploma for all to see. To me that would be very humiliating, so I had decided to skip the graduation celebration, spare myself the embarrassment, and give the impression that I would be on vacation at that time.

My overall grade was 2.32, which wasn't very good considering that the highest grade was 1.00. To enter middle school I had to have between 1.00 and 2.00. My worst grade, 3.50, was in algebra. Years later I went to college and received a degree in electrical engineering. So I took a weakness, mathematics, and mastered it, majoring in a field where it was essential for success.

As the weeks passed, little by little I became more familiar with this new country. I noticed the fevered activity of New York City. It seemed that all people were working to make something out of themselves. That's what I wanted—to make something out of myself.

I realized that I had to become responsible for myself. My family was no longer around. If I were to become something, it was up to me. My future was in my own hands, and, if I prepared myself properly, I would be able to take advantage of opportunities as they came.

What I needed first was to learn English.

In my search for a quick method to learn the language, I enrolled in a special class for foreigners at a local school. However, for some reason, the word "foreigner" didn't set right with me. Although I was in this country on a student visa, I had decided that I wanted to be an American—not a foreigner. I wanted to belong to the American way of life. So, how could I really feel that I belonged to America if I considered myself a foreigner?

The English classes were too slow for me; I needed to learn the language quickly. Eventually I learned English by attending movies. In the movie theater I normally didn't understand enough English to be able to follow the story line; however, by watching the actions and listening closely to the language, I knew that there was a correlation between the two. What could be better than to listen to the language and at the same time watch the conversation acted out?

I was encouraged by the prospect of having found a way to learn English. There was light at the end of the tunnel. It didn't take more than about four to six weeks to substantially increase my vocabulary. But that required at least twenty hours a week in the movie theater. I wasn't particularly interested in what the movie was about; my main interest was to listen and learn.

Those words whose meanings I didn't understand I filed away in my mind, hoping to bring them back to memory later. There were always questions I had about the people, the culture, and the language of my new country.

But there were idiosyncrasies with which to cope. I had difficulty buying apples by the pound, when "pound" is spelled "lb." So, you guessed it! The first time I bought apples I smartly walked up to the grocer and said in "fluent" English, "Give me one lib of apples." He quickly corrected me. He said, "It's pronounced "pound." While munching apples, I knew I would have some difficulties with this crazy language.

The transition from a European to an American had to be a quick one. I was finding that it was just as difficult for me to put on the mantle of the American as it was for me to shed my European feathers. But above all else, one realization helped me make this change: this was a country full of energy and opportunities—a country that was willing to help anyone who, in turn, was eager to put forth some effort to reach a goal.

As I began to recognize something of the pulse of this land, I saw a people who were going somewhere. And I was going to join them. Here was a nation, I felt, that had a mission to accomplish; it had the resolve to rise above the tragic circumstances of the 1930s and take its place among the people of the world.

This country to which I had come revealed its subtle faces. It was so much different than I had ever thought it to be. Here wealth and poverty lived next door to each other; joy and despair were neighbors. Many nationalities met here and started to understand each other and the world in which they lived. Here was a culture built by everyone contributing something from their own rich background.

Wherever I turned, a different country met me, greeting me with smiles and encouragements. At every turn the message was the same, "Welcome, make yourself at home."

As I look back now, I still don't know why the passengers on the ship which took me to America had experienced such a different response from the people than I had. Over the many years that I have lived in the United States, I have found that the friendliest and most helpful people in the world are right here in this wonderful country.

I had come to America all by myself as a boy and had hoped that I would never again have to travel like that. Nevertheless, my lonely journeys were far from over, and I'd have to become a man now, responsible for my own future.

Chapter Three
Something to Stand On

Hitler's army invaded Norway on April 9, 1940. I had escaped with only two-and-a-half months to spare. My family was still in Norway and I was very concerned for their safety. The Nazi scourge changed millions of people's lives, and mine was one of them.

The first and most immediate impact upon my life was financial. My mother had arranged for a letter of credit from which I could draw money, but the invasion caused these assets to be frozen. Suddenly, all my worldly wealth totaled $50.00. And if that weren't enough, I was unemployable because I had only a student visa and was not allowed to work. If I were to survive, it meant getting a job; and if I were to be able to stay in the United States, it meant getting the proper paperwork. Were I to fulfill my dreams and ambitions, I must find a way to stay in America.

My immediate priority now was to obtain an immigration visa. To do that, I was advised, I had to travel outside the territorial limits of the United States where an American consulate would be able to grant me a valid immigration visa. My brother Sam, who had arrived on the last ship from Norway before the invasion, agreed that this would be a good course of action for me. He had obtained a scholarship from the University of California, Berkeley, and finances would not be a problem for him.

Soon after Sam arrived, he and I were able to rescue the family treasures that the U.S. Customs officials had taken away immediately upon my arrival. The sealed trunks were filled with mostly silver—tea sets, candelabras, and the like. We stored them for safe-keeping until the war ended, with plans to eventually send them back to my mother in Norway. With that portion of my mission finally accomplished, I turned to the more pressing matter of my future.

I no longer remember why, but I decided to go to Cuba instead of Canada to get my visa.

My diary for May 5, 1940, reads: "Left New York at 5:00 p.m. and arrived in Washington, D.C., at 5:00 a.m." I was on a Greyhound bus bound for Miami, Florida. Again, I traveled alone, uncertain about what I might find around the next bend. As I continued on to the south, Sam turned westward toward Berkeley, where I planned to join him after solving my visa problem.

As we traveled through Virginia, I saw some of the most picturesque scenery of this whole journey. One setting in particular has remained etched in my mind over the years. The bus drove slowly through Richmond that morning and, as it turned a corner, I noticed a red schoolhouse on a small hill. Outside, a group of schoolchildren and their teacher, with joined hands, were singing and skipping around in a circle. The scene was so peaceful and restful; it looked as if it were a picture painted on a green lawn and then framed by large trees.

For a moment the realities of my personal quest for

survival and the horrors of war in my native country faded. I thought how nice it would be if everything in life could be as peaceful as that scene on the hillside.

When the bus arrived in Florida, regiments of palm trees lined the streets like soldiers on parade. I had enjoyed the palm trees in the Palm Garden restaurant at the Britannia Hotel in Trondheim, Norway, but this was the first time I had seen them in their natural habitat. I was awestruck by how majestic and regal they stood.

The farther south I traveled, the warmer it got. In those days there was no air conditioning on the bus. I had never experienced such a warm climate so early in the year. At home, it would have been chilly with snow still on the mountains. Summer in Trondheim arrives toward the end of June, and before you have time to get used to the season, it's gone again.

I arrived in Miami at noon on May 7. My ship for Havana didn't leave until 7:00 that evening. I was able to place my luggage in a locker at the Greyhound bus station, with plans to pick it up before I caught the ship for Havana. Since I had some spare time, perhaps I could find a bank that would cash my letter of credit. After all, I thought, Miami is so far from the mainstream business activities of New York that they might not be so aware of world conditions. I entered the first bank I saw and presented my letter of credit from Norway. The clerk took one look at it and told me they couldn't help me. My heart sank to the bottom of my feet, and slowly I walked out. I tried several other banks, but it was always the same answer. What was I to do?

While having lunch, I decided to inquire at any other bank I could find; there certainly was no harm in trying. Maybe, just maybe, one of the banks would take pity on me and redeem my letter of credit. I didn't give up easily.

Lunch over, I went from one bank to the other and presented my letter of credit while explaining my situation. In an hour's time it seemed as if I had visited every bank in the city but always with the same answer: "Sorry, we can't help you."

It was time to catch the ship for Cuba, so I found the Greyhound bus station and retrieved my luggage, which also included my heavy winter overcoat. I didn't know what to do with my overcoat. For some reason I was embarrassed that I had a winter coat in such a warm climate. How could I carry it on board? The best thing I could think of was to wrap it in some newspaper that I found on a bench and then tie the whole package with heavy rope, which the ticket clerk gave me. It never occurred to me to carry my overcoat over my arm like normal people would do.

At 6:30 I arrived on the pier. People were already boarding the ship. I was surprised to see how well-dressed they were. Some of the ladies were even wearing fur jackets. In the 1940s Cuba, I learned, was a favorite vacation spot for many people. It was inexpensive, with good service and a very pleasant overnight journey from Miami on a first-class ship.

I presented my ticket to the agent and boarded the ship, carrying in one hand my overcoat wrapped in newspaper and my suitcase in the other.

Arriving at my cabin, I was delighted at its roominess; it even had a private bath. Ships this small in Norway didn't provide such luxury. Finally, the ship cast off and began its journey to Cuba. The vacationers on board were happy and carefree, but that didn't lift my spirits. Here I was, traveling again to another foreign country all by myself. My stomach was churning with worry. Gazing across the water, I wondered what was going to happen to me when there were so many uncertainties ahead. I had become very serious about life.

After dinner, I found my way back to my cabin and quickly slipped into a deep sleep. It had been a long and tiring day.

The next morning I was awakened by a commotion. Shouting seemed to come from every corner of the ship. I hurriedly dressed, wondering what the furor might be, and rushed out the cabin door to investigate.

Many of the passengers had gathered on the top deck watching something in the water. To my relief it wasn't somebody overboard. I discovered fifteen to twenty young men in the water calling out to the passengers to throw coins. I watched in amazement as the swimmers, amid smiles and laughter, would dive and recover each sinking coin. They surely knew how to swim and appeared at home in the water. It was a pleasant and entertaining spectacle. As I watched, my thoughts drifted back to our summer villa, my birthplace in Vikhamar, a small settlement by the Trondheimsfjord, not far from Trondheim.

Every year while growing up, my summers were spent at the villa, swimming, playing soccer or bridge. Not a care in the world. Often I would spend as many as four to five hours frolicking in the fjord.

I was brought back to the present as the ship docked at the pier in Havana. I disembarked and was met by an agent from the National Jewish Council. He drove me to my hotel, and then to the American consulate.

I was encouraged because he assured me that I wouldn't have to wait very long for an immigration visa because the Norwegian immigration quota probably wasn't filled. He was right. After a physical examination, I was told my permanent immigration visa would be ready the next day.

The agent was kind enough to drive me around in the city, and we stopped at several souvenir shops all operated by German Jews. For the rest of the day I saw and heard about human tragedy. This was the time when thousands of Jews had fled Germany to escape Hitler's death camps. Many found refuge in Cuba, settling there until they could get credentials to enter the United States.

The German immigration quota was so depleted that many had to wait in Cuba for years before they could leave and be reunited with their families in the United States. So they engaged in whatever type of business or profession that was open to them. Many of those who spoke Spanish with enough fluency to be understood contributed to the economy, arts, and sciences in a more direct way.

It was a very difficult time for these people. Families had been broken up, part of them in Cuba or the United States, and another part still in Germany — their fate unknown. Others had family in South America — all waiting for the day when they would see each other again. I talked to several German Jews and felt very sorry for them, but I was unable to help them or give any word of comfort and encouragement. Comfort to them was to be united with their loved ones; and encouragement, the receipt of a valid U.S. immigration visa.

My visa was ready for me the next day as I entered a crowded room at the American consulate. I felt very fortunate. German Jews were waiting for a quota number so they would know how many years they had to wait before they could enter the United States.

While standing at the counter for the clerk to get my

final documents, I was approached by an elderly man. He was short, had a white mustache, and his suit and hat were crumpled as if he had slept in them. He asked how long I had to wait for my visa. "Only one day," I told him. Suddenly he became very excited. Waving his hands, he talked louder and louder, saying that obviously something was wrong. He had been in Cuba for two years and there would be at least another year before he would be given an immigration visa. "How did you get a visa overnight?" he asked. He was hoping that the immigration quota had changed.

I explained that as a Norwegian citizen I had applied under its quota which was not yet filled. Therefore, I got my visa very quickly. The voice of the elderly gentleman registered resigned disappointment. He slowly walked over to a worn chair and slumped down. This tragic scene has remained in my mind all these years.

I left the American consulate clutching these important documents. They were more than a simple visa which would allow me to earn a living. They were my renewed hope and an opportunity, after the required five years' waiting period, to become a citizen of the country which offered me a new life.

I had been thrust from the security of a large, well-to-do family in Norway to a strange country and language. Here I was all by myself, in a very precarious and uncertain situation. However, the immigration visa gave me something solid on which to stand.

That evening I left for Miami on the same ship which had brought me to Havana the day before.

On board ship I met two young musicians who played with the Cincinnati Symphony. They knew I was traveling alone, so they befriended me. They told me that upon arrival in Miami they were going to stay for a week at the Colony Hotel, right on the beach. I blurted out that that would be very expensive. They said it would cost them only $1.25 a day, which included breakfast. That was almost as cheap as the room I had at the YMCA in New York. They asked me to come with them and stay a few days before I continued my travels. After a little thought, I agreed.

It had been the custom for all Miami hotels to close for the summer because it was too hot for the ordinary vacationer. But this year a few hotels had decided to remain open. It was cheaper for them to do that than to have to go through the expense of hiring a new staff and cleaning the premises.

Early the next morning the sound of the ship's air horn heralded our arrival once again in the United States. The immigration officials boarded the ship immediately. I knew they would interrogate me and inspect my papers before allowing me to leave the ship.

Breakfast was served, and I remember that I ordered a waffle. But I was so anxious and fearful of all the uncertainties that I couldn't eat it. I left the table and nervously waited my turn with the immigration officers. It was at times like this that being alone was so frightening. Fortunately, my visa was in order and everything went fine with the immigration officials.

Upon being allowed to re-enter the country, my first concern was to find Sam, who should have arrived in Berkeley by this time. Prior to leaving New York, we had agreed to meet at the International House in Berkeley. But he promised that he would try to have a letter waiting for me in Miami at general delivery upon my return from Cuba. Spending a few days at the Colony Hotel with my friends from the ship gave me the opportunity to check the post office every day for news from Sam. His letter never came. After ten days, I decided to go on to California.

For the first time since news of Hitler's invasion, I had enjoyed a renewed spark of hope for the fulfillment of my dreams and a future in this country. But that momentary joy was tempered by a foreboding concern for Sam as well as for my mother and other relatives facing the uncertainty of that war so far away, yet so close to my heart.

CHAPTER FOUR
THE LAND OF FULFILLED DREAMS

A new life awaited me. Day by day. Step by step. It was a slow, arduous, and lonely journey. Yet, I held no illusions about the task in front of me. If my dreams were to be fulfilled in this, my new country, I'd have to make them happen. That meant hard work, sometimes backbreaking work, but to me the rewards were worth whatever the sacrifice.

The bus was hot and uncomfortable. It was late afternoon of May 17, 1940, when I boarded the Greyhound bus which would take me from Miami to California—a five-day trip.

As the landscape outside my bus window rolled by, my mind brought glimpses of my family back in Norway. This was Constitution Day, a day of great importance to all Norwegians even to this present day. A day of parades, band music in the streets, and long speeches commemorating the approval of the Constitution on May 17, 1814.

But this year there would be no celebrations. Norway was occupied by the Nazis, and the occupation forces forbade patriotic demonstrations. They demanded allegiance to Germany and to their cause, an order which most Norwegians ignored. I learned later that though there were no parades, speeches, or any other public festivities, many Norwegians met secretly and defiantly celebrated this holiday.

As the bus finally rolled into southern California and northward through the valleys toward the San Francisco Bay, I was amazed that my previous idea of what California would be like was so inaccurate. There were lush, green valleys where produce crops were growing, but I saw no palm-lined streets like I had seen in pictures. Evidently the route my bus took missed all those sights. Instead, the hills were golden brown because the area was going through a drought that season. What surprised me the most was that so much of California was desert.

May, as I remembered it in Norway, was a very colorful month. The countryside was covered with a blanket of deep green vegetation. Wild flowers added to the beauty and enjoyment of life; the birds welcomed another spring after a long, hard winter. Everything was saturated with the fragrance of spring. Flowers pushed up through the soil; trees showed new life—spring could be seen charging in at full speed.

May was the time of year when my family would take the automobile out of winter storage and drive to our country home at Vikhamar. It was the first opportunity to visit our summer home on the banks of the fjord. We always closed it up from fall until spring, and there was much to do to get it ready for summer. Everybody worked. The windows were washed and opened to air out the stuffy, stagnant rooms. Amidst all this the food was unpacked. We always brought a large supply of food and strong coffee when we went to the country.

This was a day that was always filled with laughter and happy sounds in anticipation of the fun and carefree days ahead of us. Soon summer would come. With school out on Midsummer's Eve, the rest of the summer was spent at my beautiful and restful birthplace, Vikhamar. But now all that was very far away. I was in California.

Arriving at Berkeley, I was disappointed by the dried-out hillsides all around. I suppose that I had expected California to be more like Florida. I didn't know it then, but California was going to be my home for thirty years. Finally, I was reunited with my brother at the International House at the University of California.

In looking for a job, I was faced with the cruel reality that I didn't have any skills. Although in Norway I had been in training for a short while to become a dental technician, I didn't know enough to qualify for a job. A kind man offered me employment when he saw my plight. For ten cents an hour I washed bottles in his small winery. I was happy to do the job but knew this was only the beginning of my work career.

A few weeks after I had started, the union official demanded that I join the union. My employer told him it was only a temporary job, but it didn't matter. He had to let me go because he didn't want to get into trouble with the union. He later invited me to dinner at his house for he knew I didn't have a place to call home. When I left that evening, he gave me several streetcar tokens which I could use when needed. I shall always remember this kindness and the concern he showed toward me.

A few days later I was hired to dig up someone's backyard. It was a backbreaking job, but I got paid for it. Next, I had a one-day job cleaning out a synagogue prior to the High Holy days. After that, I worked for a general contractor for two weeks.

I was beginning to wonder if that was all I could do. I wanted a job with a future. Then the Jewish relief agency I had been working with sent me to a men's furnishing store in Oakland called Money-back Smith. For $12.00 a week I was hired to be a stock clerk. My duties were to receive the incoming goods, put prices on them as directed by the manager, and put the goods on the shelves in the stockroom. I worked in an un-heated part of the basement, but I didn't mind these conditions. I was happy to have the job.

I rented a room at the YMCA within walking dis-tance. All my meals were eaten in restaurants or coffee shops. Breakfast consisted of two eggs, hash brown potatoes, toast, orange juice, and coffee, and it cost me 15 cents. That came to $1.05 a week plus 35 cents in tips. Then there was lunch and dinner. A five-course dinner could cost as much as 50 cents. I couldn't af-ford all these high-priced meals, so I bought a quart of milk, a quarter pound of butter, and a loaf of bread and had breakfast in my room. There was no refriger-ator, but in my dark, cool closet the perishables would last for three days. By following this routine and by skipping lunch, I was able to make ends meet on my salary.

I had no social life. I knew no one, except my brother and one fellow at work, Harold Johnson, who befriend-ed me. But usually on Sundays he was busy with his family, so I seldom saw him except at work, and Sam was busy with his own activities.

Sunday was a day I didn't look forward to. I was alone all day from the time I got up, through breakfast, lunch, and dinner. No one to talk to, no one with whom to take a walk. My English was still very poor. I couldn't even start a conversation, much less maintain it. There was just too much about the language I didn't know. So, who wouldn't be bored to death spending a day with me, I thought. I would often walk over to Lake

Merrit, stroll around it, and observe what was taking place. Families gathered there for picnics and play. Children waded in the shallow end of the lake. Young and old were having fun. I saw it all, never taking part in it. There were also trips to museums or libraries, but I never met people.

The old European school was still in me—never speak to a stranger unless you have been properly introduced. I didn't realize how free the people in America were. Making friends was no problem for them evidently, but it was for me. I found it difficult to meet strangers and make friends. How could I start a conversation? What would I talk about? So by necessity or perhaps choice, I spent many hours among throngs of people, yet alone.

Once a fellow at work said he was going to a picnic on Sunday and asked if I would like to come along. Of course, I agreed. He was going to pick me up in his car at 10 o'clock Sunday morning at the YMCA. I was in the lobby waiting for him long before the appointed hour. Ten o'clock came, then eleven. Finally at noon I knew that he wasn't coming. I had so looked forward to it—something to do other than spending another day alone.

Trying to forget my disappointment, I got up and went for another lonely walk. How could anyone promise to meet me and then break the appointment without even calling. To me an agreement was of great importance, and whenever I made a promise I would do my utmost to keep it. If I couldn't keep an appointment or would be late, I'd call and explain. As it turned out later, when I asked him, he said he had just forgotten.

After that unfortunate experience, I became a little cautious when anyone made a promise to me. I looked forward to Mondays when I would be with people at the store.

My preference was to work out on the floor as a salesman in this men's store, but the manager wouldn't permit it. My English was too poor. He was right, of course.

Working here wasn't so much different from my father's business in Trondheim. There the whole family was expected to work in whatever department they were needed. Retailing could have been an obvious career choice for me. But I hadn't considered this to be a skill.

After seeing how the men's store here in America treated its older employees, I had second thoughts about a career in this field. Two men who had been with the company for many years were discharged. Everyone suspected management didn't want to have to pay them retirement benefits. Privately, one of these men advised me not to make retailing a career. I agreed.

I knew if I were to amount to something, to make anything out of myself, it was going to be up to me. I noted with interest an item in the local newspaper—an advertisement for a Los Angeles trade school that taught radio and electricity. "Electronics" was not a trade known about by the layman in those days. I decided to enroll in National Schools on 40th and Figueroa Streets, and so I moved to Los Angeles. I could do this because the Norwegian government-in-exile in England had re-established its banking system, and my letter of credit was honored. There was enough left in the account to carry me for a year at National Schools.

By this time, an older brother, Julius, a dentist, had come to this country, and he was living in Los Angeles.

At first, I stayed with him in his little bungalow, taking a streetcar for an hour to school. After a few months, Julius joined the Norwegian air force in Toronto, Canada. I found a boarding house within walking distance of the school. While Julius was in Canada, he sent me $300.00 to help with my expenses. But once again I was all alone.

In the classroom I struggled hard with both the technical terms and the English language. I understood so little of the scientific terminology that I had to memorize many pages of the textbooks. This way I could work with the information in my mind until it made sense to me.

Toward the end of the course I had to make another decision. An instructor at National Schools told me if I intended to pursue this technical field, math was essential. Math?! My downfall in primary school had returned to haunt me. It didn't take me long to make that decision; there was little choice. I wanted an education in a technical field. That meant more study.

I spent almost every evening in my room doing homework. My life was very lonely. There was little time to socialize and make friends. I would have to continue this life style, however. It was the requirement for achieving my goal.

For a 50-cent registration fee and a dollar for the textbook, I became a math student in the evening adult education classes at a local high school.

With the course at National Schools completed, I got a full-time job repairing radios. Then, three times a week, from 6:30 to 9 p.m., I attended math classes. For the next year I spent every evening after work completing math assignments. I repeated them over and over until I fully understood the process involved in solving mathematical equations.

With few friends and no family around to encourage me, I had to find inspiration from within. All through this lonely, demanding period, something was always in the back of my mind: if I were to see my dreams come true, I would have to prepare myself for the future. I received hope and encouragement from my math teacher, Mr. Bland, a quiet, unassuming man with a receding hairline and neatly trimmed black mustache. At the end of that first semester, he looked over my work and told me that I had good potential. He predicted that I could eventually become an electrical engineer. His confidence in me was very important. His words inspired me to set my goals higher. I eventually finished the math courses at night school and from that experience saw that there was more to preparing for the future than I had realized.

The need to prepare myself for the future had inspired me to press ahead. Next, I sat in on an evening class in basic engineering at the University of Southern California and studied physics on my own. The more I thought about engineering as a career, the better I liked the idea. It appeared as if it would be a unique and challenging profession.

But how? I had no money to attend college. Even if I had the money, I didn't know enough English to pass the entrance exams. I wanted to become an engineer, but I had no idea of how to accomplish it. All I had was a desire, a dream. I needed an opportunity. That was just around the corner—somewhat disguised.

The day after the Japanese attacked Pearl Harbor, I tried to enlist in the armed forces. I visited every branch of the armed services and was told that only American citizens could enlist. At that time, it would have taken four more years before I could apply for citizenship— that wouldn't be until 1945. I could, however, be drafted. I registered at a draft board and was classified 1A.

Now all I had to do was to wait for the letter from the government beginning with "Greetings." I expected that letter to arrive the next week or no later than two weeks. But weeks turned into months and I kept waiting. Other fellows my age had been called into the service within weeks after they had been classified 1A. I worried. Perhaps the draft board had thrown away my records. Maybe they didn't want me.

August 14, 1942, came and I celebrated my twenty-first birthday—alone. This was an important event, but I had no one with whom to share it. I took the streetcar to Hollywood, went to a restaurant for dinner, and then out to a movie. I had fantasized about having a party for my twenty-first birthday: a few fellows and girls going out for dinner and dancing afterward. But, of course, it didn't materialize. I had acquaintances, but no actual friends. I was disappointed that there was only one person present on my birthday—me.

I continued working in the radio repair shop, waiting eagerly for the draft notice to arrive. Each day brought disappointment. May 1943 arrived and still no letter.

Finally in June the letter came. I was drafted. I was overjoyed and couldn't wait to tell anybody who would listen that I was going into the service. I quit my job, packed what little I had, and put it in storage.

On the appointed day I went to the induction center and took the physical. While waiting for the results, I was asked by a man in uniform what branch of the service I wanted. I thought quickly. I knew all my family members were in the Norwegian army or air force. I also knew that to get into the U.S. Navy I had to be a citizen. So I requested to be in the navy, knowing full well that I would be refused and, therefore, be put in the army. But this was my way of registering my preference.

Before long the results from the physical came back. I was told I was a perfect specimen. Before I could leave, I had to find out what branch of service I would be in. The officer who looked over my papers remarked that I wasn't a citizen, to which I agreed. In my mind I saw my whole navy career, which hadn't even started, go to the bottom of the ocean. He replied that two weeks earlier Congress had passed a law which allowed noncitizens to be drafted into the navy. I hadn't planned it that way, but there I was, a seaman. My orders were to report in five days to Union Station in Los Angeles and be shipped to Farragut, Idaho, for basic training.

I arrived at Union Station early. While waiting for the train to leave, I took a stroll around the station and saw mothers, wives, and girl friends saying goodbye to their loved ones. I witnessed an emotion-filled scene. Goodbyes were exchanged over and over again, tears wiped away from concerned eyes, some of the recruits tried to smile as if they were just going on a picnic and would soon be back home. But all knew this was no picnic, and there was no telling when—or if—they would be home again.

It filled me with sadness. I didn't like seeing loved ones separating. I remembered when I said goodbye to my mother and how both of us cried. I also felt sad and alone because I had no one saying goodbye to me now. It was the same feeling that I had upon my arrival in New York when there was no one there to welcome me at the dock, when there was no one to say goodbye to me when I left Miami for Havana, and when I left Miami for California.

"All aboard!" I climbed on, still feeling sorry for my-

self, and soon the train pulled out. I was glad we were
finally under way.

The next morning all of the recruits got off the train
and assembled on the platform. I began hearing orders loud and clear. "Get in line and no talking!
Everybody march in a military manner! No straggling!
Wipe that smile off your face!" the uniformed man in
charge shouted. I fell in line with the others, and we
followed the one in charge to a large building. Once
inside we were told to disrobe, put our clothes in the
suitcase we had carried from home, and make out a
mailing address to the place it would be mailed. I sent
mine to my brother Julius who was now in Toronto,
Canada. The navy took care of the shipping.

That finished, we were all there in our birthday
suits—waiting for the next command. In a few minutes several sailors took our measurements for every
piece of clothing we needed, from underwear to shoes.
All my measurements were put down on a piece of paper with my name on it, and I was told to stand in a
specified line that they pointed out. I was issued underwear, socks, shoes, work and dress uniforms,
several white hats, a pea jacket, hammock and sea-
bag, plus two mattress covers—and, of course, a pair
of leggings. The issue of all these supplies took place at
breakneck speed. If something didn't fit right, I was
told I'd either grow into it or it would shrink—in time.

"There is no time to waste. Get your work clothes on
as fast as possible, and line up outside the building."
The one calling out the commands counted out 150
fellows, told us to line up in four rows, and look smart.
We became Company 451, Camp Waldron.

We were assigned to the top floor of a two-story bar-
rack, told to put on leggings and fall out on the
grinder—a common name for the exercise and parade

ground. Ten minutes! Leggings in boot camp was the
distinguishing mark of a new recruit.

Out on the grinder I stood at attention while the company commander, a first-class boatswain's mate by the
name of Snodgrass, inspected us. He constantly shook
his head as if to say, "What a motley crew I have to
work with." But I was as proud as a peacock. I was in
the service, the U.S. Navy, and serving my new country. I shall never forget that first moment in my navy
uniform. I felt as if I had just received the Nobel Prize—
that's how proud I was. This was my country. I was
proud to be part of it. I was happy to help fight for it.

For the next six weeks the grinder was to be the
main theater of operation for me. Here I marched with
my company for many hours until I knew what "right
and left flank" meant as well as "about face," "forward
march," and finally "companyyyyyyyy HALT!" The most
cherished command was "fall out," which meant "dismissed."

Within days after arriving, my company was given a
battery of aptitude tests which would indicate in what
area each of us could serve best. With all my math and
physics background, I scored high in the technical
tests. All of us with high marks were ordered to take a
second test which, if we passed, would allow us to attend what was at that time the top-secret radar school.
Radar was the frontier of technology in those days.

On the appointed day a number of us from many
different companies assembled in a large classroom.
We were all eager to take the test. Before the exam was
passed out, the young officer-in-charge stated that all
those who didn't have a high school education might
as well leave because the test was so hard they
wouldn't pass. It would be a waste of time to try. Two
young men got up and left. Obviously they didn't have

a high school diploma. I didn't have a high school degree, but I knew that this young officer didn't know that. So I remained. Out of 150 men in my company only five of us were qualified to take this second test. Only three of us—including me—passed. I thought to myself afterward how important it was never to give up just because someone suggested you might fail.

For the first half of that six-week training program, we were kept in quarantine in case any infectious disease should break out. Afterward my whole company was placed on special duty for one week. Some had guard duty—twelve hours on and twelve hours off. Others had duties in the mess hall, such as washing the huge pots and pans, cleaning the "deck" (that is the navy term for floor), and other equally "challenging" jobs.

I was the only one in my company who could swim proficiently. That was lucky for me because it led to an attractive duty assignment: life guard in the indoor Olympic-sized swimming pool for the week. It was July and extremely hot, but I didn't feel any of that heat sitting poolside in my trunks.

At the end of boot camp the entire company split up. Some went to specialized schools. Most were assigned to a ship. I was waiting for my name to appear on a list which would transfer me from Farragut to the radar school. After almost two months the transfer finally came through. It had taken that long to gather enough recruits who were eligible to make up a fifty-member radar class.

The first phase of radar school lasted six weeks and was conducted in Michigan City, Indiana. The second phase, a three-month course, was in Washington, D.C., where the navy immediately began the weeding-out process. Every morning we had a one-hour math class followed by a one-hour test. Two or three times a week for the remainder of the course, an officer would interrupt our classes. He would call out several names. They were told to pack their belongings and be ready to ship out. We assumed that they had failed the exams. This procedure started in the second week of training in Washington, D.C.

During those three months we never knew from day to day what grades we made or whether we would be there the next day. This made the entire stay very intense and stressful.

At the end of the three months only 50 percent of the original class remained. Those of us who survived were shipped out to Treasure Island in San Francisco Bay to begin the third and final phase of training. At the end of this six-month phase we graduated.

Because of my European background and my knowledge of Norwegian and German, I requested duty in Europe. The navy responded by sending me to Stamford, Connecticut, for further training. A vacant retirement home for veterans from the Spanish-American War was used for this purpose. The navy had formulated a new plan. Communications units were formed consisting of several radio operators, one cook, one motor mechanic, two clerks, one technician, and two officers. The purpose of these units was to go in on the first wave of an amphibious attack and set up radio communications between the beach and the flag ship. Special waterproof, lightweight equipment had been designed which would be carried from the landing craft to a safe place on the beach.

Practicing with this equipment, I was able to set up the transmitters and receivers and have them in full operation in less than ten minutes. I was instructed to start unpacking the equipment as soon as I left the landing craft so that no time would be wasted in starting communications with the flagship. In addition to the equipment I would also carry a rifle and ammunition. It all sounded like a movie script, but the training officer stated repeatedly that when the time came, it would be for real.

There were no landing crafts on the beaches of Connecticut, so we were assigned a jeep and a location on the beach. Each morning we drove out there, I set up the equipment and watched over it for the whole day. If anything went wrong, I had to repair it right then and there. After four months of intensive training, my unit received transfer orders. But not to Europe—to California. Finally, after a thirty-eight-day journey in a convoy from San Francisco across the Pacific Ocean, I landed in the Philippines—Memorial Day 1945. I remained there for the duration of the war.

All through my naval career I seldom heard from my family who had escaped for safety to Sweden, where a sister of mine lived with her husband. In one of the few letters from home I learned that my other sister in Amsterdam had been arrested by the Nazis and with her husband and little daughter was sent to a concentration camp in Czechoslovakia. Fortunately they escaped the death camps.

When I came out of the navy in 1946, receiving my honorable discharge at Lido Beach, Long Island, I found an apartment in Flushing, New York. There I cooked, cleaned, and lived all by myself.

This was a different and better life style than I had experienced for three years in the navy, but it was still lonely. I was responsible to and for no one except myself.

Sometimes I wondered what married life would be like; however, I was in no position to seriously consider such a move. I had plans to go to college and nothing was to interfere with my education. Although I had no immediate prospect for a wife, I determined that marriage had to wait until my college years were over.

With the G.I. bill available for my education, I immediately started looking for a college to attend. This was the opportunity I had been waiting for to help fulfill my dream of becoming an engineer. Now the door was open and I was anxious to enter.

I searched through information on colleges at the New York City Library and mailed over thirty inquiries to selected schools asking for admission. While waiting for the replies, I enrolled at New York University and studied English literature. At least I wouldn't be wasting my time, and this course would be a preparation for my approaching college days.

One by one I received the replies—all negative. Openings were reserved for their returning students and local residents. This was understandable and only fair, but nonetheless very discouraging.

I became desperate. I rushed back to the library. Opening the college reference book I started at the beginning. The name California State Polytechnic School seemed suddenly to jump out at me. I hadn't noticed this school before. It described a four-year college of engineering and agriculture. I didn't go any further. Deep down I knew I had found what I was looking for.

I rushed off an inquiry for admission for the fall semester. Within a week I received a reply that there was room for me and that I should submit the required paperwork. I had been accepted at a college! Now I could pursue my dream.

I was glad I hadn't given up after the thirty rejections. I determined to learn from that how important persistence is, no matter how impossible or discouraging the situation might appear at the time. Like Winston Churchill who said, "Never, never, never give up," I was about to take another step toward my goal because I had been persistent. If I hadn't returned to the library that day in April 1946 and searched for another college, the opportunity of becoming an engineer might have passed.

In September 1946 I started college in San Luis Obispo, California. It had been in 1942 when I first dreamed of becoming an engineer, and now, four years later, I could see it beginning to come to pass.

My education had top priority. I studied hard but enjoyed college immensely. It was the first time since arriving in America that I had anything resembling a social life although at first it was very minimal.

During the four years at Cal Poly, I shared a dormitory room with another student. The room was no larger than those I had occupied in the YMCA in New York and Oakland, so a small room was no problem for me.

Every Saturday and Sunday I stayed in my room studying. The only luxury I allowed myself was a once-a-week dinner in a local cafe followed by a movie, usually on Saturday night. The first two years in college I had no transportation except for the local bus. Later, I bought a '34 Chevrolet coupe for $150. It wasn't much of a car, but it was all mine and paid for. A year later, in my senior year, I traded it in for a '42 Graham-Paige, four-door sedan—a powerful car with a supercharger. Driving up Questa Grade, a steep, long hill north of San Luis Obispo, I passed every car on the road at eighty miles an hour.

I organized the Cal-Poly Ski Club and became its first president. Today it's the largest club on the campus. I joined the Men's Glee Club and was an active member for four years. At one time I even ran against two other candidates for student body vice-president. Two of us tied with the highest vote. In the runoff election I lost.

Many of the students held jobs on campus to supplement their income. I was among those who worked in the cafeteria for their meals.

I enjoyed all my classes, but I still had difficulty expressing myself. So I enrolled in a public speaking class. I was scared when the instructor assigned our first exercise, which was to give a one-minute talk on any subject.

The class was instructed to know the material, to prepare in advance what to say, and then to say it with conviction. When appropriate, we were to add some humor. I discovered it wasn't so scary after all. I even enjoyed it.

I learned to be ready for many opportunities and challenges, and not to be afraid to become involved with something I knew very little or nothing about. I could always learn. There was, and still is, no weakness in admitting there are things I don't know.

Those college years were some of the happiest I had ever spent, but it pales in comparison to what was about to happen. In my senior year a wonderful young woman came into my life. Could this be the end to my loneliness?

CHAPTER FIVE
HELLO, DORIS —
GOODBYE, LONELINESS

Like a feather floating in the arms of a gentle breeze, she danced across the room. Her red kerchief skirt and white peasant blouse flowed with her every move. Her golden blonde hair reflected the bright lights. That was the first time I saw Doris. It was at a folk dance in San Luis Obispo.

I danced past her, unable to take my eyes away as she twirled across the floor with her partner. I enjoyed what I saw and wished I could meet her. But how? I was far too shy to simply walk up and ask her for a date. There had to be another way—and there was.

Bill, my roommate, was dating Doris' sister, Virginia. In November I started urging him to arrange a date for me. It wasn't until the following February that our first meeting took place.

It happened like this. Bill and I planned to take the sisters to the Valentine's dance on campus, quite appropriate I thought for our first meeting.

From the very beginning I found Doris different from the few other young ladies I had dated. She was so easy to get along with, and I didn't have to search for things to say—words came easily. Unfortunately, that first evening flew by like a minute. Doris, who had studied ballroom dancing with a professional, was an especially good dancer. And, at least in my opinion, I was, too. I often thought it curious, however, that she never made mention of it.

For me that first date was a wonderful time of discovery. Her every word exhilarated me. The conversation as we danced was far from romantic, but we were getting acquainted and I enjoyed that. As she talked, I learned more about her. She lived with her sister and two other young women. All except Doris were schoolteachers. They lived in a rented house in Santa Maria, a small town about thirty miles south of San Luis Obispo. Doris worked for the local phone company.

When she told me that each week one of the four was in charge of buying the groceries and cooking the meals, I thought I saw an opportunity and seized it. I learned that next week it was Doris' turn to shop. Neither she nor her sister had a car. Whenever they went to the grocery, they had to walk, carrying heavy bags on the return trip. From time to time they'd stop, put down the bags, and rest their arms.

After the dance Bill and I drove our dates home to Santa Maria in my 1943 supercharged Graham-Paige. Before Doris went inside, I asked if I could see her again. I told her I could come down the following Saturday and drive her to the grocery store. She accepted. We said good-night at her doorstep.

I could hardy wait until Saturday, but it finally came. Buying groceries turned out to be fun. Doris read the labels on every item she bought. I asked why she did all that. "So I'll know what's in the food," she answered. To help, I started reading the labels, too. But this seemed like another foreign language to me—I didn't understand what all the ingredients meant.

On our first date alone I took Doris to dinner. Afterward, she invited me into her living room where we listened to classical music and talked about many things, including music. I told her I was especially fond of Mendelssohn's Violin Concerto. By our next date Doris surprised me by buying that recording and playing it for me. It was a warm feeling sitting with someone I cared about and listening to my favorite recording, a recording I hadn't heard since leaving Norway. I realized for the first time just how very kind and considerate Doris was.

These were happy times. The days turned into weeks and weeks into months. I was growing more and more serious about Doris but didn't know if she shared my feelings. I devoted myself to studying and attending classes during the week, but come Saturday afternoon I was on her doorstep.

During those times together I learned more about Doris. She was born in Huntington, West Virginia, where her parents still lived, and she had three sisters and a brother. Her father was a plumber; her mother was very musical and had also taught herself oil painting. Their family background was German-Dutch on her mother's side, and French, English, and Scotch on her father's side.

The three oldest daughters—Sita, Virginia, and Doris (in that order)—were very active in their church. They sang in the choir, and Doris and Sita were often called on as soloists. Music, in one way or another, kept the sisters busy all through their school years. Sita studied art, piano, and organ and became very skilled in all three. Doris told me of warm memories of her home when Sita would play the piano, and the family enjoyed countless hours of songfests.

I was a dry riverbed and Doris, a spring shower. Her

stories of home and family filled me with a seemingly insatiable need to hear more. She told me of her experiences during World War II, when the choir wrote the story and music for a cantata and performed the production at their church. Sita helped compose the music, and each person in the choir wrote her own part in the play; there were no young men in the choir—they had all gone to war.

Doris and her sisters enjoyed these opportunities to sing. A sextet of the three sisters and other members of the choir was formed. They built up quite a repertoire and were invited to sing at meetings throughout the city and at garden parties.

Doris also sang in the high school choir and played the viola in the school orchestra. She had even entered a radio talent show and won a prize. Later, the station received a call from a New York theatrical agency which had an office in Huntington. They offered Doris a professional contract.

But as it turned out, show business was not for her. She made one professional appearance. It was a variety show at a convention in Wheeling, West Virginia. On her way home Doris confided to her mother that the kind of atmosphere she witnessed backstage was not anything that she would want to experience on a regular basis.

Her talents also included acting. During Doris' senior year in high school, she performed in a local little theater's production of *Rumpelstiltskin*. The production with very extravagant costumes and sets had been staged in schools all over the city. A gold light was used to highlight Doris' blonde hair, and for a couple of years after that children who recognized her as "the golden lady" in *Rumpelstiltskin* would stop her on the street.

All those experiences gave Doris a sense of who she was and confidence in her capabilities. Sharing these vignettes of her past gave me an insight into this young woman who was becoming more and more fascinating to me.

After finishing high school in 1946, Doris enrolled at Marshall College, but a year later she moved to Washington, D.C., and took a job at the Pentagon. When her sister, Virginia, accepted a teaching position in California in the fall of 1949, Doris decided to accompany her on this new adventure. That's when she took a position with the local telephone company. In her spare time Doris sang now and then on the local radio Sunday morning inspirational program and performed in a weekly radio drama group. These activities were my main competition when I first met her.

Knowing these details about Doris helped me understand her and gain a deeper appreciation for her. While we had obvious differences in terms of culture and heritage, I chose to focus more on what we shared, such as her love for music which matched mine, plus our mutual fondness for biographies and poetry.

It didn't take long after meeting Doris for me to realize that I had fallen in love with her. We dated for two months before I summoned the courage to tell her how serious I was. The fact that she was surprised, in turn surprised me. It was a great disappointment for me to discover that she didn't feel the same way about me. She assured me that she thought I was a fine person, and she confessed enjoying my company. But she hadn't considered it any more than that. She wanted more time to see if our relationship would blossom.

I didn't like it, but it made sense.

We dated every Saturday, becoming better acquaint-

ed. She was quiet and thoughtful, and her behavior
was consistent with good manners. It became a joy for
me just to be with her.

My love for her grew very rapidly. I was happy simply to be in her company. We would take long walks, in
the rain or sunshine, sometimes without speaking a
word. To know that she was by my side, to feel her
presence, just the two of us listening to the silence
together, were very comforting and peaceful moments
for me.

During our long talks I noticed how attentive she
was to what I was saying, never interrupting with
something she wanted to say. I knew I had much to
learn from her in the way of patience.

As time passed, I became more convinced that Doris
was the woman I had been dreaming of. I had been
waiting and looking for someone like Doris for many
years. In her I found the answer to the longing of my
heart. Now I hoped my dreams would be fulfilled.

I told her that when I first started college I would
often pray that God would bring me a young woman
whom I could love and who, in turn, would love me.
Doris understood. For years she also had prayed for
the young man she was to marry. We had been on the
same wavelength.

Even then, I felt that Doris was building my identity
and security simply by being with me. Whenever we
talked about the future, she would always encourage
me to do my very best and reach for the stars. Often
she would say to me, "A man who is capable of doing
more is never satisfied doing less." That touched a re-
sponsive cord within my being. Over the years this has
helped me understand myself on a deeper level.

We not only came from different countries and
cultures, we also came from different religious back-

grounds. During our dates we talked about our family upbringing and what we did on the holidays. Doris told me about the Christmas celebration in her family: opening the gifts on Christmas Eve, singing in the cantata at church, and celebrating Christmas Day with a special dinner. It all sounded cozy and friendly.

I told her about being Jewish and that we didn't celebrate Christmas. Instead we observed Chanukah. My father would light the eight-armed candle holder, one candle the first night, two the second, and so on. While the candles were lit, we sang a song in Hebrew. We never exchanged gifts. Christmas Eve was a very quiet time for our family and for Trondheim. The streetcars stopped running at 5 o'clock, all the stores were closed as well as theaters and restaurants. The hush over the city was broken only by the ringing of the church bells calling the parishioners to the special Christmas Eve service.

She told me about the Depression days and how her father had waited in the bread line for a sack of flour, corn, or whatever the government gave out so that he could feed his family. It hurt his pride to get something for nothing, she said, and I felt a deep sympathy for him. Rather than taking what he thought was a handout, he was willing to sweep the streets to earn the cost of the food.

Doris explained that everyone around them experienced the same difficult times. My heart went out to those who had endured such hard times. I had never experienced anything like that myself. In the 1930s Norway was spared the economic depression, and my family was comfortable. The contrast was a revelation to me.

Doris and I shared a lot of fun memories. What could be more pleasant than to be with the one I loved? We

were serious about our relationship and had many discussions about philosophy and hopes for the future.
But we laughed a lot, too. Sometimes in private moments I would act like a comedian to entertain her.

While in the company of others, it was as if we were
completely alone, just the two of us. Together, we
dreamed of the future. Even so, she still hadn't made
up her mind about our relationship.

Graduation from college was an important event for
me, but of equal importance was learning if Doris
would marry me. By May I had enough courage to ask
her again. I was afraid that she would need more time
to think it over. But to my amazement and delight she
said "Yes!" I believed it would be a great and wonderful
life to be married to Doris. And it has been.

She never suggested that my being Jewish might
put an obstacle in the marriage. We knew that we had
at least the foundation of believing in the same God.
She accepted me for what and who I was, and I did the
same for her, though we knew there might be challenges because of the differences in our religious
backgrounds. I wondered how my family and hers
would accept our marriage. She could feel that concern. But from the beginning, her family accepted me
with open arms. In fact, when we were on a picnic with
her parents, who were visiting from West Virginia, her
father handed me the keys to his brand-new car and
told me I could drive them home. I hadn't asked for
that. I didn't realize the significance of this until Doris
told me that he would never trust his car to anybody,
and handing me his keys was his way of giving me his
stamp of approval. With the exception of two brothers,
my family never did accept Doris, and this has been a
lingering sorrow in my life. In spite of that, it has been
a very rewarding and beautiful relationship.

I had met Doris in February of my senior year, and in June my days at Cal Poly would come to an end. It had been quite a challenge, but finally I had my bachelor of science degree in electrical engineering. Of the 150 students in my freshman class, only fifteen of us were to graduate. From the time I arrived in the United States in February 1940 to the day I was to graduate from Cal Poly in June 1950, just over ten years had passed.

On Saturday, June 2, 1950, I received my diploma. Doris made a surprise trip from Santa Maria to attend the graduation exercises, and she was the only one present on my behalf. I had no idea she would be there because I assumed she was without transportation—but she found a way. It was such a joy to see her in the audience. She had bought a new dress for the occasion, white organdy with green polka dots, white hat and gloves, and matching shoes.

Over the years I had become used to being alone at important events in my life. Now, I no longer felt lonely, nor alone. It was comforting to know that someone in the audience cared. From that time on we have been together.

Originally, we had planned a December wedding, anticipating spending our honeymoon in the snow country somewhere in the mountains. I had already made reservations at a lodge at Big Bear Lake, California. But that wasn't to be. As a naval reservist, I was called back to active duty during the Korean War, so we moved up our wedding date to the second of September 1950.

Through these years of marriage there have been problems and disagreements, but we have found a way to work them out before the day is over. Doris always said that we mustn't let the sun go down upon our wrath, and we have tried to live up to that. I have come to love Doris with a capacity I didn't know existed within me. Each morning as soon as we are awake, our first words to each other are, "I love you!" And at night these are the last words spoken before we go to sleep.

CHAPTER SIX
STARTING OUR
SPIRITUAL JOURNEY

Married life was even more delightful than I hoped it would be. But I had much to learn, and Doris was a willing teacher in many areas of my education. Although I had recited prayers from my childhood on, I was about to discover the power of prayer—and that was an initial step that moved my life in wonderful and unexpected directions. Doris led me to this threshold as together we embarked on an exciting spiritual journey.

But Doris was more to me than a companion and teacher; she was my partner, and I was no longer lonely. I had someone to come home to and someone with whom I could share my dreams, hopes, problems, and disappointments. Doris filled the longings of my heart. Life was rosy.

Of course, there were many adjustments to be made. Every decision that either Doris or I made would affect both of us in some way. Doris had always lived with either a sister or a friend and was more accustomed to considering the needs of another. The greatest difficulty in adjusting was on my part, for I had lived by myself for so much of the time since I left Norway.

Now, I had become one with Doris, and as much as I wanted to include her in all aspects of my life, it took a conscious effort to do so, some careful attention to be thoughtful. But since I had been so lonely for so many years, these adjustments were the ones I joyfully and gratefully made.

Doris and I were eager to share our lives and thoughts with one another. She cared about how I was doing wherever I was, and I was interested to know all about her day. As we asked questions of each other and shared our experiences, I was aware of how much my life was now changed.

After finishing my second stint with the navy, I started a new job in the Los Angeles area, and Doris and I settled into married life. We bought our first home in Lakewood, California, on the GI Bill of Rights—with $500 down. It was a real mansion, we thought—three bedrooms and a bath. Even though our home was in a good neighborhood and my job challenging, the hour-long drive to and from my office in Los Angeles in nerve-wracking, bumper-to-bumper traffic each way began to take its toll on me.

Finally, I had had enough. I came home one day and told Doris that I was quitting. I wanted to move to a smaller community. But where? Engineering jobs in small towns were scarce.

Doris understood my frustration. She encouraged me to start looking for another job. There was no question in her mind that finding a smaller area to live in would be much better for me. She suggested that we pray first before starting on our search. I had never done anything like that before, but felt it probably wouldn't do any harm.

Doris believed that we should be very specific in our prayers; in other words, we should have in mind some definite ideas of what we needed before we made our request known to God. Together we planned what to pray for, and all through those difficult times Doris was very gentle and so very patient. I marveled at how anyone could show these traits so consistently through such trying circumstances. I was upset and worried about our situation. Doris was calm.

So we prayed. We made our request known to God. It had three distinct parts: We wanted to live in a small community, close to a larger city, and have a ten-minute drive to work. That was it—short and to the point. We were very specific.

Doris and I didn't sit and wait to see if God would answer our prayer without our doing anything. In the process of doing what we could, we believed God would lead us to the right place at the right time. So the next morning we drove north, checking out every small town for an engineering position for which I might apply. We found nothing. Unfortunately, there weren't any small towns close to a large city, except San Jose and other small towns near San Francisco. That option wasn't any better than Los Angeles as far as I was concerned.

Nevertheless, when we returned home, we started to pack our household belongings and put the house on the market. We still had no idea where to go if and when the house sold. One day while packing, I had an urge to drive south to San Diego. Hurriedly we prepared for the trip.

Early the next morning we were on our way, and I contacted Ryan Aeronautical Company in the San Diego inner harbor. After reviewing my credentials, they offered me a position. I accepted on the condition that I could find a place to live near the office. The personnel officer at Ryan knew of an apartment in Ocean

Beach. He said it wasn't far and gave me explicit directions how to get there.

In the meantime, Doris had been waiting for me out in the parking lot. The minute I returned to the car she exclaimed that this area might be no better than Los Angeles. With this she pointed to the bumper-to-bumper traffic. I reminded her that if the distance in that traffic was short I wouldn't mind it. I told her about the apartment in Ocean Beach.

Ocean Beach—we had never heard of it. Our experience in California had taught us that the name of the city was no assurance that it would be factually descriptive. Just because the name had "ocean" in it held no inherent guarantee that it was anywhere near a beach or the ocean for that matter. For example, we hadn't seen any river near Riverside, California. So for all we knew Ocean Beach could be in the middle of the desert.

We drove along Harbor Drive, crossed Rosecrans Boulevard, and up Narraganset Avenue. The car climbed the steep hill and at last came to the top. Spread out before us and below us was the Pacific Ocean. What a beautiful sight! We stopped and took it all in. The ocean was as quiet as a mirror and, though it was early October, we saw several people swimming. Everything looked too good to be true. But it *was* true and it *was* good.

"So this is Ocean Beach," I said to Doris. The hillsides were dotted with well-kept homes surrounded by beautiful gardens. Everyone in this area obviously had either a green thumb or a gardener. Wherever we looked there was an abundance of vegetation. Fragrances of jasmine and honeysuckle saturated the air.

As we looked down to the street below, it was as if it were calling to us, "Don't stop now, you are almost home." We found the apartment, and it was less than a block from the cliffs above the beach. But how could we be sure that this was the right place? I can still remember how we sat on the front lawn considering the possibility of moving there. While we were quietly talking it over, we could hear the ocean breaking against the cliffs. It sounded like a team of horses as the waves came galloping in with full force, charging against the cliffs, only to slip quietly back out to sea and return for another attack. It was very invigorating. I thought that this would be a really desirable area in which to live.

But, more important, I wanted to be sure that this was what we'd asked for in our prayers. It seemed perfect. I wanted to believe that it was the right place, but I had some doubts. What if it weren't? We would be spinning our wheels. The only thing to do was to find out if any of the signposts we had asked for in prayer were present: live in a small town, close to a larger town, and ten minutes' drive to work. The landlady might know some of the answers.

We talked to her and found out that Ocean Beach— whose one main street was only four blocks away—certainly fit the description of a small town. What's more, she told us that San Diego was twenty minutes' drive away. Two of the three criteria we had asked for were right before our eyes.

There was one more aspect of our request that had to be checked out. We needed to have all three parts of our prayer fulfilled before we could accept this new area as the answer we had requested from God. Two out of three wasn't good enough.

I asked the landlady if she could hold the apartment for thirty minutes. We wanted to check out something, we told her. Driving from the apartment to the entrance gate of my new employer took exactly ten minutes. God had answered our prayer to the minutest detail. With excitement, we rushed back to the landlady and rented the apartment.

Two weeks later we moved to Ocean Beach.

While living in the apartment, I asked Doris to be on the lookout for a suitable house to buy. We had just sold our home in Long Beach and had taken a second trust deed from the buyers. We didn't know how we could finance another house at this time but wanted to see what was available. It took six months for her to find something that might be of interest to us. When I came home from work one day, she told me she had seen a house which I might like.

I was reluctant, actually, to go out to see the house at this time, but Doris insisted—in a kind way—that we should go immediately, even though I wanted to have dinner first.

Five minutes later we were on our way. When I first saw the house, it looked like any ordinary, garden-variety home. But when the lady of the house opened the front door and I looked in, all I could say was a loud and surprised "OH!" She invited us in and we entered a tropical garden which was surrounded by the kitchen, living room, and main bedroom. A major portion of the construction consisted of floor-to-ceiling windows, with open beam ceilings throughout. It was in a quiet neighborhood up in the hills and just the right size for us. The owners wanted $13,500. For us it might as well have been a million. We liked the house and wanted to have it. But how?

We called the real estate agent and told him we liked the house but the mortgage payment, property taxes, and insurance could not be higher than $125.00 per month. Then we prayed and presented to God what we had found, and the terms we had set. If it was His will for us to buy the house, would He cause the terms to be accepted by the seller? If it was not His will, we wouldn't want the house at all. However, we reminded Him that it was even two minutes closer to work!

The real estate agent was a "horse trader" of sorts. He was able to put together a deal we couldn't refuse, and together with the second trust deed from the Long Beach house it was within our financial capabilities. All we had to do was to sign on the dotted line.

We loved our years living in Ocean Beach. Occasionally, however, I would become discouraged because situations in my office didn't work out the way I had hoped. For example, once after I had been in a discouraged mood for several days, Doris quietly asked me to go for a drive with her. I agreed. She drove to a movie theater saying that she thought I would enjoy seeing the film *A Man Called Peter.*

That movie inspired me and lifted me immediately out of my depressed state of mind. To this day I'm very thankful to Doris for being so alert to my needs. But that's the kind of wife Doris is—always considerate, always giving of herself.

In the winter of 1953 I enrolled at San Diego State College to pursue a master's degree in engineering to be followed by a Ph.D. in the same field, specializing in engineering management. All the courses had been agreed upon by my advisor, and I spent most of my time after work in evening classes or studying at home. I recalled that I had done the same while living in Los Angeles in the early 1940s, but now I had Doris to come home to instead of being alone.

I also began to think about the career impact of higher degrees. The highest position I could achieve would be president or even chief executive officer of a large corporation. That would be challenging. Later, after further thought, I wondered, "What else is there to achieve beyond that?" At that time my only interest in obtaining advanced degrees was to enable me to excel in my field. Surely there must be more to life than that. But what? No matter how successful a position the material world could ever possibly offer me, still I could see that it wasn't going to be satisfying at a deeper level. Something vital would still be missing in my life.

I saw that deeper level as something having to do with God. Though Doris and I had been guided by God to Ocean Beach, I hadn't become religious in any form or way. Nevertheless, from my early childhood I had felt a deep inner pulling toward God, but had been afraid to let it surface lest I be made fun of by family and friends. Now being no longer influenced by the family, I determined to give myself wholeheartedly to God. This resolve came without any lights flashing before my eyes or sensations going up and down my spine. I didn't hear divine voices. Everything appeared to be the same as it always had, except that now I was confronting a very intense and empty void within. This had gone on for several months after I began my master's degree program, and I didn't know what to do about it.

In discussing this with Doris, she suggested we attend a church on Sundays and a synagogue on Friday nights. I agreed, though I couldn't see what that would have to do with my inner problem. We attended services in these two houses of worship for several months, but nothing of what I heard filled that empty, hollow void within me.

In fact, a more private approach to spirituality had been the only thing that had worked for me, so far. I recalled that when I was in the navy during the Korean

War, I found a Bible and often read from the Gospel of John, Chapter 14, verses 1-6 ("Let not your heart be troubled . . . "). I noticed that these words brought much comfort to me. My need was great then because I was lonely for Doris, and I felt that opportunities in the engineering field were slipping away as long as I was in the navy.

When I was released from active duty and reunited with Doris, the void temporarily disappeared. However, the emptiness surfaced again, and this time it stayed with me. I couldn't understand it. I had a wonderful wife and home life, and a good job which was only ten minutes away. So why wasn't I satisfied?

I decided to take matters into my own hands and join a synagogue. That was the only thing I knew to do at the time. I felt I had to do something. Besides, the synagogue was my background. Making the necessary inquiries opened my eyes to something I wasn't aware of: a membership fee of $75.00 for each person, plus additional fees for attending the High Holidays. While listening to this information, I quickly calculated that for Doris and me to become members would cost us at least $150.00 a year, but to belong to a church would cost us nothing. The answer to me was obvious. I could enter the synagogue and still come out spiritually empty, which would be quite costly. But I could enter the church and leave spiritually empty for free. We dropped the Friday evening services at the synagogue and continued attending church on Sundays.

Though we didn't become members, we were very active in the church. This included joining the choir. Doris became assistant choir director, director of the youth and children's choirs, plus becoming active in the missionary society. Together we also were sponsors of the youth group. However, I noticed that all this activity didn't fill my inner void.

My colleague at the office, Mike Hammond, was very perceptive. He had noticed my frame of mind and one day asked me about it. Very cautiously I felt him out to determine if he could be trusted and initially gave him a less-than-frank answer. This deep inner void was something I didn't talk about to anybody except Doris. But over the next several weeks I observed him, wondering if I dared open up to him. What if he betrayed me? Finally I decided to share with him what was going on within me. He listened and then related how he also had experienced these feelings but had found a solution: he had experienced a personal relationship with God through Jesus Christ, and that encounter had filled his inner void and changed his life completely.

Well, that was all I could take. I was crestfallen because I had hoped for a solution that would fit my need. I listened to him in silence and made no reply other than to excuse myself. If that's the answer for him, I thought, God must have another one for me, for as a Jewish person I needed a Jewish answer.

To consider having a personal experience with Jesus Christ was out of the question for me. The church Doris and I attended turned out to be more of a social club. The sermons were about current events. Once in a while God was mentioned. I found nothing offensive to my Jewish background in it, but to have a personal experience involving Jesus Christ was another matter. Hadn't my people, the Jews, been persecuted for centuries by those who named the name of Jesus Christ? So why should I become one of them? This was just too much for me. I became very fearful.

Even though I was far away from family influence, I couldn't help wondering what my mother and brothers would think if I made such a commitment. For years my father and all my relatives had warned everybody in the Jewish community in Norway to stay away from Christians because they persecuted the Jews.

When the Nazis occupied Norway during World War II, each soldier wore a belt buckle with the inscription "Gott mit Uns" (God with us), and the Nazis, who called themselves Christians, were in the business of exterminating the Jews.

From historical records I had learned that the established churches in Spain and Russia at one time had given the Jews an alternative: either kiss the cross of Christ and be converted, or be executed in the name of the Father, the Son, and the Holy Ghost. While still living in Norway, I had heard stories about some Jewish people who had accepted Jesus Christ as their Savior and their family had committed them to an insane asylum. Also, I recall how my younger brother and I were taunted in public school by classmates who followed us yelling, "Christ killers!" Obviously, Jesus Christ couldn't be the answer for me.

I told Doris about my conversation with Mike, and she understood my fear and apprehension. She never pushed me into making a decision that would make me feel uncomfortable.

CHAPTER SEVEN
THE AWAKENING

Several days later Mike asked if I would mind a friend of his, John Marshall, coming over to my house to explain the historical and religious impact of Jesus Christ. I couldn't understand what this other fellow could tell me that I didn't already know from my upbringing. Nevertheless, I agreed.

The evening with John was spent with him reading to me from the Old Testament. It was the part of the Bible with which he thought I would be familiar, and he offered his interpretation. After he had already read several passages, he began one which I assumed was from the New Testament because it seemed to refer to Jesus Christ, although that name wasn't mentioned.

When he finished, I pointed out that the last passage wasn't from the Old Testament but from the New. He corrected me by saying, "You're right that this passage speaks of Jesus Christ, but I was reading from the prophet Isaiah, Chapter 53." Then he showed it to me, and in amazement I read it myself.

Before John left, he urged me to accept Jesus Christ as my Messiah. With emphatic words I said I couldn't do that because this was too important a decision to make on the spur of the moment. However, I did state that the only one who could convince me about Jesus Christ was God, not any human being. If God would show me that Jesus Christ was my Messiah, I would accept that answer. Doris suggested that I make it a matter of prayer, and I agreed to this. With that John left.

I had made a promise and I was going to live up to it. So that night I prayed that God would show me if Jesus Christ was my Messiah, and if not, I wanted to be shown that, too. For six nights I said the same prayer before going to sleep. Nothing happened. I wasn't any wiser about the answer and wondered how much longer this was going to take. Then on the seventh night I got my reply.

I dreamt that I was in a large room with many people. Suddenly, the scene changed and I was now walking with Doris down a dark, empty street. I looked at my watch and it was three minutes to twelve. I knew that the end of the world was coming at midnight, and my first thought was that I had to be baptized. (That had not occurred to me before.) We rushed back to the room we had come from; and when we entered the room, I saw in the far left corner a man I knew was a minister—one who could baptize me. As Doris and I approached him, she disappeared. I knew she had gone to heaven. I wanted to go with her, so right then and there I said, "I take Jesus Christ as my Savior." Immediately there was a warm feeling that started at my heart and flowed to every part of my body.

I sat up in bed, awakened Doris, and told her what had happened in my dream. Unfortunately I didn't have the presence of mind to look at my watch. If I had, I'm sure it would have said 12 o'clock.

The next morning I felt as if I was on my way to

recovering from a long illness. My knees were even a little shaky. I couldn't maneuver very well and my thoughts were caught up with the dream. What did it all mean? Where should I start in order to find out?

I couldn't reconcile my Jewish heritage with the thought that I had to be baptized. For a Jewish person to *convert* to Christianity was bad enough. But also to be *baptized* to confirm his faith was the last straw. Back in Norway I had heard how a Jewish family had conducted a funeral service, with burial plot and grave marker, when one of its members had been baptized into the Christian faith. It wasn't that I wanted my family to believe like I did, nor did I seek for their approval. All I hoped for was that they might accept me for who I was and for the decision I had made.

I considered myself still a Jew and always would be, no matter what I believed. I would like to have had my family see it the same way. The whole morning was occupied with these thoughts. But in spite of all this, I considered the dream to be the answer to my prayer. Though there were doubts and fears in my heart, I knew I couldn't reject what God had shown me so clearly in my dream. As I considered it more and more fully, I realized it was telling me that my old world was coming to an end at midnight and something new was about to begin in my life. I had to find out what that could be.

I had promised John Marshall I would pray until I received an answer and would let him know what it was. So there it was, and I had to act on it. I phoned him to share this experience. He invited us to a Bible study group which met in his home every Friday night. Neither Doris nor I had ever been to such a group, and we felt a little uneasy as we entered the Marshalls' home the following Friday night. But we enjoyed the

Bible study so much that from then on we couldn't wait until Friday night rolled around.

Shortly after my dream experience about Christ, I went to the minister of our church and told him about it. He advised me to do nothing for six months and then it would go away. For a moment I was stunned by his reply. It seemed that he was negating my experience. I confided in John Marshall about this, and he suggested I find a church whose minister would be more sympathetic to my experience.

I invested in two new Bibles—one for each of us—and we started to read. But there was so much we didn't understand, and I wanted, of course, *immediate* knowledge and wisdom. Seemingly in response to my desire, a wonderful opportunity was presented. A missionary named Grace, whom we had come to know at the Friday night Bible class, offered to come to our home weekly and give us private Bible instruction—a class for just Doris and me. We jumped at this wonderful proposition. We promised to commit ourselves to this class for three months, and during that time we wouldn't allow anything to interfere with it.

At the first meeting Grace told us that most of the promises in the Bible aren't for our time here on earth, but instead will be fulfilled when we get to heaven. I didn't know anything about promises in the Bible, so I didn't discuss that with her. I just wanted to get on with the Bible study.

For the next three months Grace was an excellent teacher, covering every facet of Christian belief. She taught the cardinal doctrines that I must believe in order to be a knowledgeable Christian. Of course, that's what both Doris and I wanted to be.

I was especially interested in her teaching of eternal hell for those who don't accept Jesus Christ as their

Savior in this life. As she put it, there is only one life and after that the judgment. She also taught us about the nature of God—His love for humanity and how He cared for it. And we heard about the evil of humanity, and that all people need to repent and come to Jesus Christ.

I asked her about those who had never heard what we were now being taught. Would they end up in hell? She indicated that they would. But she also said that God's mercy would bring them to repentance if people would only listen. This troubled me and I raised a question: If there is no one to tell them, how could they know to repent? She replied only that "they'll know," and then the subject was changed. Years later, such an incomplete answer wouldn't have sufficed for me. But for now I accepted the viewpoint of those who seemed to know lots more than I did. In turn, I came to be a teacher and defender of this belief—often in a determined and obnoxious way. I probably offended many people with my beliefs but that, I was told, came with the territory.

In addition to teaching the Bible, Grace also pointed Doris and me in two directions: to set up a family altar and to find a church home where we could serve and discover our ministry. I had no idea what she meant by a "family altar" or by us "finding a ministry." She didn't explain because she probably assumed that I already knew. I didn't want to show my ignorance, so I asked no questions. Only later, as we got more deeply involved in church life, would we discover what she meant.

With the Bible classes over, we felt very happy with all the biblical knowledge she had given us and were now ready to take the next step. We decided to look for a church that would be sympathetic with my experience.

After visiting a number of churches, all belonging to the fundamentalist persuasion, we eventually became members of Brooklyn Heights Presbyterian Church. A new page of our growth was ready to be filled.

The minister, a tall slender man with graying hair, was a friendly and loving person. He carried himself with great poise and dignity. His sermons were inspiring and delivered with beautiful oratory. He welcomed us into the fellowship and encouraged us in our spiritual growth. Soon we were fast friends and maintained that friendship for many years. Often I would meet with him before the Sunday morning service and we would pray for the needs of the church.

We became involved in their visitation program and made weekly visits to shut-ins. We always prayed for them, asking God's blessing and healing power to descend upon them. The church held a weekly prayer meeting which we attended faithfully.

After a short while, I was asked to teach an adult Sunday school class. That became a challenge for me. They had been members of the church for many years, and I was a little apprehensive since they probably knew much more than I did. What business did I have teaching them? I thought it should be the other way around, and I admitted it. Nevertheless, they were gracious people and insisted that I would do fine. We enjoyed our Sunday mornings together.

It was soon thereafter that I discovered the meaning of a family altar. I overheard the minister talk to a young couple about establishing one. Fortunately for me, these people didn't know what a family altar was either, but they had courage enough to ask him. The minister spoke of establishing a daily time for quiet Bible reading and prayer—a private time with God. The mystery of the family altar was finally solved, and Doris and I immediately decided to keep a regular family altar time in the mornings.

Early in this quest I determined to be committed to God, and I saw the family altar as one way to fulfill this. I didn't believe in doing anything half-heartedly. In my case it was either total commitment or none. As I was introduced to this new and extraordinary world, a fascinating and better life began to form within me. The inner void had been filled.

I enrolled in correspondence courses from several Bible schools. I wanted to know as much as I could about God, so I spent a great deal of time completing these courses. With every assignment a new light was shed on the many attributes of God. I discovered a God who was good, caring, kind, and loving. What was especially rewarding was that both Doris and I enrolled in these courses and worked on the class assignments together. Side by side we became more knowledgeable about God and His nature. One of our favorite Bible verses at that time was "That I might know him, and the power of his resurrection, and the fellowship of his sufferings, being made conformable unto his death . . . " (Philippians 3:10)

During those early months of our spiritual journey, Doris began encouraging me to share with others our experience and discoveries. This built my confidence as friends began to listen. Whenever a discussion led up to something in which we had specific knowledge or experience, instead of sharing it herself, Doris urged me to give an explanation.

As I look back, I can now see that she was purposefully "pushing" me out in front. She was trying to help me take my place in the world around us and to feel comfortable in it. What's more, as Doris and I became more proficient biblical teachers and as the minister in our church saw how knowledgeable we both were in the Bible, we were invited to be speakers at church retreats.

I hadn't forgotten Grace's instruction that most of the biblical promises won't be fulfilled until we get to heaven. I couldn't figure out why some of the promises had to wait. I needed them right now—right here on earth.

Doris and I talked about it, and we decided to test some of the promises to see if they would work in the here and now. I was very impatient and wanted immediate results. No sooner had we decided to test them out than an opportunity presented itself.

An evangelist was holding a series of revival meetings in San Diego, and we decided to attend. At the first meeting he opened his sermon with the subject of the promises of God, stating that they were for our time. That sounded like good news to me! For the rest of the evening he preached on one specific promise: "Give, and it shall be given unto you; good measure, pressed down, and shaken together, and running over, shall men give into your bosom. For with the same measure that ye mete withal it shall be measured to you again." (Luke 6:38)

I was determined to test this promise. To prove my sincerity before God I gave a large donation when the collection plate was passed. I expected a miracle by Friday, when the revival meetings would conclude. That was the time I had set for God to prove that this promise would work for me. Surely God would see my point and bestow upon me riches untold in just a few days.

Friday came and no great fortune had dropped into my lap. I became enraged. I told Doris I was going to the meeting that night, find the evangelist, and tell him that the promise didn't work. Doris told me to use a little patience with God, but I didn't have time for patience.

At the meeting hall I found the evangelist. Out of embarrassment for me Doris waited at the door while I talked to him. I told him that the verse which he had preached on the preceding Monday night hadn't worked. I had tested it out for four whole days and it was all to no avail. He looked at me, seeing an impatient young man, and said that I had to give God time to work things out. All I could say was that the promise didn't work and it wasn't worth fooling around with. I felt like saying that I wanted my money back but, of course, I didn't.

Doris and I stayed for the meeting, but I didn't remember anything from his sermon. I was angry because I believed that either the evangelist or God had pulled a fast one on me. So I didn't put anything in the collection plate.

On the way home Doris and I talked about my confrontation with the evangelist and how hostile I had been. We continued this discussion for several hours after we got home. Finally it became clear to me that I had the wrong attitude about giving. Doris suggested that developing a *consistent* pattern of giving might be a better test. It was difficult for me to think about setting aside a regular amount of money each month. I would have to think further about that.

If this promise of God hadn't worked up to now, why would I invest even more effort to test it? But then Doris reminded me that a farmer, before he can plant seed in his field, has to plow and fertilize it first. Then he can seed it and begin his wait for the harvest. But while he is waiting, he is wise to irrigate it and weed it. All this takes time and effort. In due season he has a crop in accordance with both what he planted *and* the efforts made while the plants were slowly growing. I could see what she was driving at. It made sense. In contrast, I had only planted my seed. I hadn't plowed, fertilized, or irrigated it with consistent giving, prayer, thanksgiving, and patience. Instead, I had planted my seed poorly and yet expected an instant bumper crop.

In retrospect I have found that the promises of God have worked wonderfully. Doris and I have enjoyed a better life and greater prosperity on all levels. We have seen how God has provided abundantly for us, proving that His promises are for today and that they work.

The idea of a family altar became very important in our lives. Now that I had a goal in mind—to experience the fulfillment of God's promises not only materially, but spiritually and physically—I determined to make time every day for prayer and meditation. So Doris and I set our alarm clock for an hour earlier and began our day with a quiet time with God. I started to experience a deeper stirring within, and together Doris and I shared what God was teaching us. Evenings and Sundays were spent in Bible study and church-related activities. I started to collect a library of religious books. Then an event took place which had a long-lasting impact on my life.

I had heard of a lady in our neighborhood who had received a remarkable healing from cancer. The one who told us didn't know her name but knew that she lived on our street. Doris and I felt that we just had to find out who she was. The only way we could imagine to find her was to go from door to door asking if there was a lady in the house who had been healed. It took a little time before we had the courage to do it, but finally we started our search.

Beginning a block away, we knocked on the first

door. Nobody there had been healed. At the third house the lady pointed across the street and told us that it was Mrs. Young who had received this miraculous healing. We went right over and knocked at her door. When she opened it, we introduced ourselves and said that we lived nearby. We had heard that she had been healed in a marvelous way. Would she mind sharing her story with us?

She graciously invited us in and told us that she had suffered from colon cancer and had undergone surgery to remove the cancer, leaving her with a colostomy. Sometime after the surgery, she attended a revival meeting where the evangelist prayed for her. From that time on her body functioned normally as though she didn't have the colostomy.

While we were exclaiming the wonder of what God had done for her, a man walked into the room. She introduced him as her husband, Colonel Young, a retired army officer. She said that his great interest was books. Perhaps we would like to see his collection. With a gleam in his eyes, Col. Young led us to the back of his house.

He was a short, somewhat stocky man in his late sixties, bald, with still a touch of red in the fringe of hair that was left. He was wearing what seemed to be his old army clothes. His walk was quick and youthful. As he opened a door, he asked us to excuse the appearance of his library. He had long ago run out of shelf space for his books.

It was a small room. The only furniture was an old-fashioned double bed, high off the floor, with lots of space under it. I could see right away that this space was filled with books. On each side of the bed, bookshelves lined the walls from floor to ceiling. The shelves were built to hold books two rows deep. On top of the bed, stacks of books covered every available space.

He opened the closet door and, instead of clothes, books in precarious stacks filled the entire space. There was hardly room enough for the three of us because books were also stacked all over the floor. Then he said, "You'll have to see this!" With an elegant gesture he opened the door to the bathroom and stepped back. I could hardly believe what I saw. The claw foot bathtub was full of books; the toilet seat cover and water tank were topped with stacks of books. Piles of books were all around the floor except for space to walk in and out. It obviously wasn't used as a bathroom. Then he ushered us out to the garage, where we found boxes on top of boxes filled with books. He had to leave his car in the driveway.

All the while we were overwhelmingly impressed with his collection and told him how happy we were for him that he could have such a treasure. We confided in him that someday we hoped to have an extensive collection of study and inspirational books ourselves. He agreed that this would be a worthwhile project for us. Then he said that he had a book he would like for us to read.

Leading us back into the bedroom, he went to the book shelf to the left of the bed. Taking two books from the third shelf, he reached in farther and withdrew from the back row the book he had in mind. He said, holding the book to his chest, "This book has been very meaningful to me. I think you would enjoy reading it." It was *The Ministry of Intercession* by Rev. Andrew Murray. I thanked him and promised to take good care of it and return it just as soon I finished reading it.

That began a long and rewarding friendship. Many a time thereafter I would visit Col. Young, and we would "talk books," as he called it. Whenever he spoke on this subject, it was as if he were sharing secrets about close and cherished friends. He spoke as if in deep thought, with carefully chosen words. Obviously, books were his favorite topic, and his detailed descriptions clearly showed how well he knew the subject. He would tell me about the authors of these books and the depths of their spiritual lives as if he knew them personally. He knew the history of every author who lived in his collection and eagerly included that information as we conversed. With each book he pointed out what I should pay attention to if ever I read it myself.

Col. Young was a remarkable man. In addition to all his church activities, such as teaching several Bible classes, he also had a photographic memory. In the course of an evening he could easily read a good-sized book and retain over ninety percent of what he read.

Once in a while he found a gem of a book which he wanted to give me. He would caress it as if it were a living thing and then, holding the book with both hands, would hand it over to me as if to say, "Read it to learn, but take good care of this treasure." I always came away from his home with a happy heart and new challenges to explore. His love for books and his contagious joy were transferred to me as an engraving upon my soul.

With Col. Young as my inspiration, I began to obtain autobiographies of historical religious leaders, an exhaustive concordance, Greek and Hebrew lexicons, and literary works by Bible scholars. I bought them from a second-hand bookstore in England through a catalog which Col. Young had given me. Doris and I referred to these books frequently to help us understand words and passages in the Bible.

Our time in the San Diego area came to a close. I had applied for and received a better engineering position in Los Angeles, and we prepared to move. We had enjoyed living in Ocean Beach so much, and it was difficult to say goodbye to the many dear friends in our church and in the Friday night Bible class. We weren't sure that we could bear to leave. These people had become our family and we wanted to stay. But on the other hand, we felt that we should take advantage of the new opportunity. We didn't want to sell our wonderful home, so we were able to lease it in hopes that we would be back soon. Doris felt that we would return in three years.

At our last Friday night Bible class, the group presented a book to us signed by all the members in the class. A Bible verse from the Old Testament was included: "And, behold, I am with thee, and will keep thee in all places whither thou goest, and will bring thee again into this land . . ." (Genesis 28:15) This was very reassuring and comforting to us because it suggested that we would return to the San Diego area someday.

Chapter Eight
Learning to Trust God

Nothing is easy, it seems, but faith has a way of seeing you through. Even when one's faith falters, God remains steadfastly true to His promises. That's a lesson I have seen demonstrated in my own life over and over again—and this new situation was no exception.

Doris and I arrived in the Los Angeles suburb of Compton, where we had already arranged to rent an apartment near my office. We expected the moving van to arrive within the next hour or so. While we waited, a man came by and introduced himself as the new owner of the apartment building. Between the time we had rented the apartment and the time we were ready to occupy it, the building had changed ownership. What a surprise when he told us that he was going to raise the rent, even though we had agreed with the former owner on a lower amount! That agreement didn't seem to make any difference with him. It didn't seem right, and I felt the original agreement should be honored. I explained to him that we couldn't afford the higher rent, and if he persisted we would be forced to find another place to live. He persisted.

Doris and I walked to the corner drugstore, and I

called the moving company, asking them to intercept
our shipment and have the van wait to unload until we
had located another apartment. The dispatcher explained that this would be impossible—he had no way
to communicate with the driver. He didn't know where
the van was. All we could do was to wait for them to
arrive at the address given. What a predicament!

Slowly we walked back to the apartment. But all the
while I felt a deep, quiet peace welling up within me.
Somehow, I knew that everything would work out all
right, but I didn't know how. Along the way back, I
prayed that we would be in God's perfect will regarding
this matter.

When we returned to the apartment, the landlord
was waiting. He said he had changed his mind. He
would honor the rental agreement we had made with
the former owner. Silently I said, "Thank You, Lord."
We had done all we knew to do and God did the rest.
Within the next hour the moving van arrived, and the
driver started unloading our furniture just as we had
originally planned.

We were far away from our friends and felt isolated.
That first Friday night Doris and I missed the Bible
class so much that both of us cried. If we could have,
we would have driven to San Diego just to be present
for that meeting. But we were now on our own. Although we missed that fellowship, we knew that we
had to be weaned from those people, wonderful as they
were, so that we could stand on our own two feet. It
was hard to accept but necessary for our own spiritual
growth. Alone in our new apartment, Doris and I had
our own time of prayer and we read the Bible. It wasn't
the same as a Bible study class, but it was the best we
knew to do.

That Sunday we found a nearby church and joined

the morning and evening worship services. It wasn't the same. I compared this congregation to the one in San Diego and was disappointed. That comparison was, of course, unfair. I realized afterward that each church community has its own personality. As Doris and I talked it over, we decided to give this new congregation a chance; after all, it was really just a matter of getting acquainted with these new church members. I knew in my heart that I should be thankful for everything, wherever I was.

As it was, my new engineering job with TRW was very demanding and kept me busy late each night designing instrumentation devices for the space industry. Soon I had little time to think of anything else except the job. Besides, I wanted God's will on everything in my life; and if God wanted us to stay in Los Angeles for the rest of our lives, we would do just that. But I hoped God had something else in mind for us—and He did.

A shock wave hit the aerospace industry on October 4, 1957. Russia launched Sputnik, the world's first orbiting man-made satellite. That 184-pound space vehicle beeped its way around the earth every 96 minutes. To paraphrase a Revolutionary War expression, this was a space-age "shot heard 'round the world." Reality sunk in; Russia had out-maneuvered the United States for space dominance. Everybody in the scientific community was stunned. What had gone wrong? We had the technology. We had the manpower. We had the expertise and know-how to launch satellites. So why had the Russians beat us? Perhaps we had been too complacent.

The disappointment and the accompanying loss of national prestige didn't dampen my enthusiasm for our space program. It would be only a matter of time, I believed, before the tide would turn in our favor.

My work was very demanding and slowly chipped away at the time I planned for continual spiritual development. Within a few months Doris and I had found a house to buy in Torrance, California. We moved again with our pet Chihuahua, Tosco, and were happy there. It was a little farther from my office but the traffic was very light all the way. I carried work home with me every night and after dinner was busy composing proposals, reviewing reports, or writing technical papers. All this kept me up late, many times past midnight. As a result, I found it increasingly harder to get up in the morning early enough to have my quiet time with God as I had hoped. I didn't think much about it, though, for I believed at that time that my job was more important than anything else. But God sent me a message.

The company announced that my division was to be relocated to Denver, Colorado, and all key employees were to be transferred. Denver was a choice area we were told. With high expectations we agreed to move, sold our house, and arranged to rent a house in Denver until we could decide in what part of the city we would settle.

It was just a few days before the scheduled move when Tosco disappeared. In an unguarded moment, the door had been left open and our little pet saw it as an opportunity to see the world outside our home. When I discovered she wasn't in the house, I walked through the neighborhood until dark calling her name, hoping she would hear me and rush back—but to no avail. Early the next morning, before daybreak, I was out on the street calling her. Again, no luck. On my lunch hour I came home from my office and continued the search. After work I searched again. The next day was a repeat of the first. Our little Tosco was still missing and moving day was fast approaching.

The next morning, before daybreak, I was calling for her on the streets. Suddenly it occurred to me that I was willing to get up early in the morning to look for a pet, but I wasn't willing to get up early to meet with God. Sadly, I realized that I didn't have my priorities in the right order.

I promised God that if He would help me find Tosco, I would get up early every morning to have a quiet time with Him. As if Tosco's disappearance had been for me to learn a lesson and get my life in order again, that same evening I found her in a nearby housing development which was under construction.

When Tosco finally heard me call her name, she appeared from an unfinished garage. I rushed over and picked her up in my arms. I was so happy I cried. Tosco was hungry, cold, dirty, and scared. I carried her, running all the way home. Doris and I gave her a bath, fed her, and wrapped her in a warm blanket. She snuggled down and fell fast asleep, knowing she was safe once more with her masters. While I was happy to have Tosco back, it made me feel guilty to realize that she had had to experience this fear and separation so that I would do what I should have been doing in the first place—making a place for God in my life.

The next morning Doris and I arose early to have a quiet time of prayer, Bible reading, and meditation with God.

With Tosco happily in tow we drove to Denver.

It was summer and the weather was hot. We were very uncomfortable. Neither Doris nor I can tolerate much heat. As it turned out, we didn't find Denver to be as attractive to us as we were led to believe. In California we had lived very close to the ocean, but in Denver we felt like fish out of water. Now we realized how important the ocean was to us.

A number of the others who also had been transferred were sorry that they had come to Denver, each
for a different reason. We inquired about transferring
back to the Los Angeles area, but the company vetoed
it. The only way to get back to the West Coast, it
seemed, was to find another job in California. Some
did just that.

However, Doris and I had prayed about the move to
Denver prior to accepting the transfer, and we were
certain that this was the right thing to do. We assumed,
therefore, that God had something for us to learn while
we were there.

Coincidentally, we discovered an organization called
"The Navigators" located in Colorado Springs, sixty
miles south of Denver. They taught people how to study
the Bible on their own. Doris and I enrolled.

Over the next three months, we gained considerable
help and encouragement as the teachers schooled us
in how to set up daily spiritual disciplines. We learned
that discipleship was not just daily Bible study, prayer,
and meditation. It was equally important to apply
God's principles to our lives through wholesome
thought, speech, and behavior. This was the beginning
of serious spiritual disciplines for us. We were convinced that this training must have been the reason I
had been transferred to Denver. We hoped that having
gone through those disciplines, God would allow us to
return to Los Angeles with the company.

At the Denver office, the project to which I was assigned was at a standstill. After three months of hectic
and intense work, the original design was found to
have a serious flaw, which caused the project to fall
behind schedule. I had an idea for a complete redesign
that would solve the problem, and I prepared to recommend these changes at the next regular project

meeting which was to be held in Los Angeles.

Before I left for the meeting, Doris and I prayed. We talked to God as we would to a highly respected friend. If we had learned the lesson for which He had sent us to Denver, please give us a sign that He was now ready to move us back to the West Coast. After this prayer, we felt we needed confirmation that we were on the right track. We decided to put out a "fleece." This approach is based on a biblical story told in Judges 6:36-40.

The method needs some explanation. God called Gideon to lead His people in the battle against their enemies. At first, Gideon resisted the responsibility because he felt inadequate. However, he knew that if God wanted him to be the leader, he couldn't fail. But Gideon had to be sure, so he devised a test for verification. At night he placed a fleece of wool on the ground. He asked God to give him a unique sign by making the fleece of wool wet, while the ground around it would stay dry.

The next morning the fleece was wet with dew, but the ground was dry. That was a remarkable answer, but Gideon needed to be doubly sure. He spoke to God again, this time asking for the reverse: a dry fleece on wet ground. Sure enough, the next morning this is what he found. For Gideon it was undeniable assurance that he should be the leader of the people.

Now facing a dilemma in Denver, Doris and I followed this principle. Of course, we didn't use an actual fleece as Gideon did. In this instance I had an idea for our "fleece." The sign would be one of the engineers greeting me in the lobby of the building where the meeting was to take place saying, "Aron, the best thing for this project would be for the company to bring it back to Los Angeles." If that happened, I knew that

God would move us back.

A few days later I traveled to Los Angeles for the important meeting. As I walked into the lobby of the building, I saw one of the engineers with whom I had worked months before. We hadn't had any occasion to communicate since I left for Denver. He walked straight over to me and said, "Aron, the best thing for this project would be for the company to bring it back to Los Angeles."

Immediately I knew in my heart that God had answered our prayer and that we were about to move. Sure enough, during the meeting my design proposal was presented, and the chief engineer announced that he wanted the project back in Los Angeles—and that he wanted *me* to come with it.

I called Doris that evening and announced, "Start packing! We have only seven days to get ready to move back to Los Angeles."

We had put out a fleece and it worked.

The arrangement was that I would be on loan to the Los Angeles division for three months. The furniture was put in storage in Denver. With our personal effects in our car, we drove to my new assignment.

Three days later we arrived in Los Angeles and found a furnished apartment in Redondo Beach near the water. We were happy to be back. Every evening after I came home from work, Doris and I went for walks along the beach. It was so refreshing and invigorating to be near the ocean again. We listened to the breakers crashing against the shoreline. It was a welcome sound.

Months went by and I was still on loan status. Eventually a permanent transfer was approved, without my having to request it. God had worked in our behalf to bring us back to the West Coast. We were ecstatic. We found an unfurnished house to lease in Manhattan Beach, brought our furniture out of storage, and moved to our new home.

Right behind our home was a church. We became active members there and taught Bible classes. Doris directed the choir. This was a very rewarding part of our lives. We continued with our personal Bible study methods, which we had learned from the Navigators, always discovering more about God. The Navigators promoted a scripture memory program which we liked, finding that memorizing meaningful Bible verses brought us closer to God. It also gave us helpful guidance for our daily lives.

The way I saw it, my profession as an engineer was a means to make a living, whereas my entire life centered around God. I applied the Bible principles as best I could to my daily life, not only at home but at work, too. I strove for practicality and balance, and I tried to avoid becoming a fanatic. These goals weren't always easy to achieve, but I made a sincere effort. Daily, I committed my life to God. To me every day was another challenge to live for God and serve God's people.

Often Doris and I visited her parents in San Diego, and every visit brought a deep longing in our hearts to return there and live in our house, which was still being leased. But when? We loved that area so much; however, we realized we needed to be careful about wanting to return so much that our will would get ahead of God's.

To make sure that this didn't happen, I avoided contacting companies in San Diego for employment. Doris and I prayed that if God wanted us to return to San Diego, He would open the door and a company would contact me.

On the surface it appeared to be a daring request. We had never prayed like that before. But most important to us was that we remain in God's will. The future, as well as the present, was in His hands. We would follow God, no matter what.

On one of our trips to San Diego, I visited the City Rescue Mission where Doris and I had once served. I saw the founder of the mission and shared with him how much we wanted to move back. He listened very carefully, and then he showed me a Bible verse: "Delight thyself also in the Lord; and he shall give thee the desires of thine heart." (Psalm 37:4) I immediately identified with the last part of the verse. To me it said that God would give me the desires of my heart which was, of course, to return to San Diego. But first I had to delight myself in God, and that put a temporary damper on my enthusiasm.

There was something I had to do first, and then God would do the rest. It gave me hope. I talked about it with Doris. As far as we could tell, we were already delighting ourselves in God. We deeply enjoyed all our spiritual disciplines. Our lives had been greatly enriched by them. We gave thanks daily for His goodness to us; we enjoyed His being with us; we daily practiced His presence as best we could; we gave thanks for everything He brought us—whether they were trials or triumphs. So why weren't we back in San Diego? Perhaps the timing wasn't right. All we could do now was believe that, as we continued to delight in God, each step along the way would be pointed out to us at the proper time.

For many days afterward, we continued to talk about the message of the verse, and we saw another meaning: God actually places *His desires* for us in our hearts when we delight in Him. Therefore, when we know we are delighting in Him, we can accept that the desires that come to us are from God. For then, God's desire is our desire.

A few days later I received an invitation from Brooklyn Heights Presbyterian Church in San Diego to speak before a men's retreat to be held in a few weeks. I accepted. I had attended their retreats years earlier and enjoyed the speakers, the fellowship, and encouragement for my daily life. As usual, the retreat was to be held in a mountain lodge far away from noise and interruptions. There we would all have an opportunity to quiet our spirits and listen to God. It was an experience I always enjoyed, and now I looked forward to another one.

During a break between sessions, a church member approached and asked if I were thinking of returning to San Diego. All I told him was that I was praying about it. On Sunday afternoon I returned home and shared with Doris what had taken place at the retreat, including the fact that someone had asked me if I would ever return to San Diego.

The next Tuesday's mail brought an application form from a company named General Dynamics/Astronautics, in San Diego. I immediately believed that it was the work of God; however, I wondered how they had learned about me. (I was later to discover that God had prompted the physicist, whom I had met at the church retreat, to present my name to his company's personnel office as a worthwhile candidate for recruiting.) I sat down, filled out the application, and mailed it the next morning. Doris and I thanked God for showing us the next step.

We waited to hear from the company.

Near the end of the week, a phone call came from General Dynamics inviting me to come in for an inter-

view. I was elated. This was the next step. Doris and I
drove down for my appointment. While I went for the
interview, Doris spent the day with her parents who
lived on the beach. The interview went well, and I was
told that I could expect to hear from them in about two
weeks. Even though no job offer was extended, I was
sure I had it. I said as much to Doris when I returned.
We sat on the patio facing the beach and talked about
packing, moving, and rejoining our friends at our
former church. It all sounded like a dream which was
about to come true. When we left San Diego we were
happy, believing full well we would soon be back to
stay.

Back at my office something new had developed. Our
division was planning to move the operation to Canoga
Park, a suburb north of Los Angeles. My division manager wanted to know if I would be willing to relocate. I
didn't know what to say, but I promised to think about
it. To heighten this crisis, the house in which we were
living had a lease that was soon up for renewal.

Close to a month went by and still no word came
from General Dynamics in San Diego. Had they
changed their minds? I was bewildered and uncertain
about the future. If the San Diego position failed to
materialize, I would have to move with my division to
Canoga Park. It was a discouraging thought because
housing costs were very high near the new office location and the thought of a long commute in heavy traffic
didn't appeal to me.

In the meantime the family who rented our home in
San Diego wanted to sign another lease—for three
years. I felt like a juggler with four bowling balls in the
air—not knowing which one to catch. Doris and I felt
very strongly that we shouldn't lease our house for that
long a term. But when the family heard our decision,

they moved elsewhere and suddenly we had two monthly house payments. But throughout these crises, there was calm and peace within Doris and me. We were confident everything would be all right. We just weren't sure *how* it would all work out.

Doris went to San Diego to redecorate our now vacant house, leaving me by myself for a week. One evening after supper I picked up a hymnal and started to sing some familiar hymns. I was seeking some comfort from the words. Without the support of Doris all the problems facing me began to build into a case of high anxiety. After all, the situation was a bit scary. Nothing was certain. I didn't know in which direction to turn. It was impossible to make any plans.

I went through a number of hymns. Then I flipped the page and started to sing "Amazing Grace." When I came to the verse which ended with " . . . the hour I first believed," it was as if a bolt of lightning hit me, speeding from the top of my head to the bottom of my feet. I stopped singing and knew without a doubt that Doris and I would indeed be moving to San Diego. In that moment, that fraction of a second, I *believed*. Finally, I knew that I knew that I knew.

I had been learning to trust God since my first encounter with Christ. But this time I felt my faith reach deeper—wider. At that instant I somehow received confirmation from God that I was on the right path and that in due time the move to San Diego would take place.

A great joy came over me. Suddenly I was as happy as I could ever hope to be. I phoned Doris in San Diego as soon as I climbed down from "cloud nine" and told her what had happened. She was equally excited upon hearing the confirmation which had taken place.

The next Friday after work I drove down to San Di-

ego, and together Doris and I started planning our
move. She had worked very hard that whole week and
the interior of our home had a certain professional
touch. The walls—which were freshly painted a pow-
der blue—felt warm and comfortable.

Driving back to Manhattan Beach that Sunday afternoon, we were both excited and concerned—excited
that I had received spiritual confirmation about our
move and concerned that I hadn't heard from General
Dynamics. Time was growing short. Decisions had to
be made—and soon. But what decision could I make?

Monday morning I was called into the manager's office and asked whether or not I intended to move to
Canoga Park. I asked for a little more time. The manager said he had to know within two weeks so that he
could find a replacement for me in case I decided not
to move. That wasn't much time and I said as much to
the manager. He pointed out that it had been two
months since the first announcement about the upcoming move was circulated, and he thought that
amount of time to be more than adequate.

As usual, I telephoned Doris at home during lunch
to find out if any letter had arrived from San Diego.
But on that day, as on other days, it was the same
answer—nothing. By Friday there was still no word
from San Diego, and I was becoming very agitated and
nervous. I began to doubt. I wondered if I had read too
much into my "Amazing Grace" experience. Could I
have misinterpreted it? Doubt and fear occupied my
mind all that day.

That evening after dinner I determined that something had to be done. Doris and I sat down to review
the situation. What were the issues facing us? The
lease on the house in which we lived was up for renewal; my manager had to know within a week if I would

move with the division; our San Diego house was vacant; and I was waiting to hear if the General Dynamics position would be offered to me. If the position was offered, we would need our home in San Diego for ourselves; otherwise, we would have to lease it again.

We considered what might be the best way to pray about all this. Doris reminded me of a principle found in I John 5:14-15: If we know that what we pray for is His will, then we know that He hears our prayers and will bring them to pass. Most of our anxieties and concerns seemed to center around the timing of General Dynamics' decision. Together Doris and I prayed that God would tell us what day He would bring the answer from San Diego. We asked Him to use the Bible to let us know. Once we knew the day, we could be praying according to His will.

We both opened our Bibles and continued reading from where we had left off in our morning quiet time. We were reading in different places—I was studying Leviticus, chapter 23, and I noticed that the fifteenth of the month was mentioned three times. To find a single date repeated three times in the same chapter was a strong indication to me that this was the date God was giving us. It now was April 10, 1959, and the fifteenth would be the following Wednesday. My manager wanted my decision no later than Friday the 17th. Doris and I thanked the Lord for showing us the exact date of His plan for us to hear a decision. For the next five days we prayed to hear from General Dynamics on April 15, and we felt very confident that it would come.

Wednesday the 15th came and, as was my custom, I called home at noon. Normally, the mail was delivered by 11:30, so I eagerly expected the letter from San Diego to be there. But to my deep disappointment

Doris informed me there was no mail from San Diego. After that somewhat discouraging conversation, we hung up the phone.

I went for a walk to clear my mind. How could I have misunderstood? It had seemed so clear and definite. I believed God and was positive that He would guide me. I believed He had given us a date. Yet, the day was here and the answer hadn't come. Could I have read into it something that wasn't there? I just didn't know.

Discouraged I went back to my office, trying to concentrate on my work. If we weren't going back to San Diego, then it must be God's will for me to follow my division to Canoga Park. And what about our empty house in San Diego? It was obvious it had to be leased out again—and soon.

By mid-afternoon I had reconciled myself to stay with this company, planning to tell the manager of my decision the following day or at the latest by Friday. Then I turned my attention back to my desk and got lost in deep thought, attempting to solve a problem that had come up on the project. My concentration was interrupted by the phone ringing. I looked at my watch. It was four o'clock. Probably some supplier, I thought, wanting to know when to ship some specially designed parts which I had ordered.

I picked up the phone, and it was Doris. She seldom called me at work, so I wondered what she needed or if there were problems at home. I was wrong on both counts. I could hear the smile in her voice as she told me that a telegram had just arrived from San Diego. I had the job!

The rest of the day was spent rejoicing and quietly giving thanks to my God. He had made good on His promise. The fifteenth was the day He had set and the answer came on that day. Yes, my faith had waned when I had thought that God was limited to the use of the U.S. Postal Service. But to my delight and surprise, God can choose whatever means He so desires to let us know His answer—even Western Union.

Certainly, this experience made the principle in I John 5:14-15 very real to me.

Together at home that evening there was a great celebration in our spirits. Doris and I were so thankful that God had heard us and had answered in the nick of time. That Friday I informed my manager that I wouldn't be going to Canoga Park, but instead moving to San Diego.

When Doris and I returned to San Diego at the beginning of June, we felt that the whole city had turned out to welcome us back. That's how happy we were.

As I grew spiritually, I learned that God's will for my life would be revealed to me in direct proportion to my willingness to listen. To stay in that will, I had to remain spiritually alert, attuned, and ready to respond. His will didn't always come in the same manner each time.

When I reported for work at General Dynamics, it wasn't long before I felt that the department to which I had been assigned wasn't using my talents sufficiently. Even though the work was interesting enough, I knew I was capable of more. I started looking for a department that needed my skills and would use my talents. Finally I found a department that had challenging work, and I was invited to transfer. But I would have to initiate the transfer through my current department manager, and, as I was to discover, success was not a sure thing.

In the weeks that followed, I realized that timing can be very crucial and that action is often required without hesitation. It became a matter of listening to inner

urges and believing that what God says is true. All that
was necessary for me to do was to follow through.

Wanting to discern the correct timing, I prayed for
the right opportunity to approach my manager so that
the transfer could be accomplished in the shortest possible time. Several weeks went by and I had felt no
inner prompting—all was quiet. Then one morning the
message came. It was while I was attending a professional conference. As was my custom, I had gotten up
early to read the Bible, continuing where I had left off
the day before. It was the story in which God tells Elijah to go and see Ahab. (I Kings 18:1-2)

Immediately I connected this scene with my situation. Ahab was the symbol of a man in high authority,
just like my department manager. God was showing
me through this Bible passage that *now* was the right
time.

When I arrived at my office, I immediately went looking for my manager; however, he was on vacation. Had
I misunderstood? Was the timing wrong? I found his
assistant instead and stated my transfer request. He
immediately agreed, asking when I wanted to make
the change. By the end of the day all the paperwork
had been processed, and I was in the new department.

Later, I learned that if I had seen the department
manager for the transfer, he would have refused it. He
was known never to allow anyone to transfer from his
department, not wanting to lose any of his people.

For me, the timing had been right. Just how effective my guidance had been all along was made evident
to me a few months later.

A sales engineer, whom I had known from my days with
TRW in Los Angeles, called on me at my office. We discussed the business for which he had come, and then
he sat back and began talking about my former com-

pany. "I see their move to Canoga Park didn't work out."

"Oh," I replied, "I'm sorry to hear that!"

He went on to say they had closed the doors after six months. Then he said with a chuckle, "You must have had some inside information." In a way I think I did. I believe that God had given Doris and me the desire to return to San Diego. It seems that He arranged it just in the nick of time. I had been protected from a big lay-off by moving.

My years at General Dynamics proved to be an extraordinary opportunity for me professionally. Aerospace had caught my imagination, and I was fascinated by the possibilities of this new technology of space travel and working with these new concepts.

In 1960 I was assigned to a team of scientists to study the feasibility of sending a manned expedition to the moon and returning the crew and vehicle safely to earth. This was the seed that grew into the Apollo Space Program, inaugurated by President John Kennedy as a national commitment to be the first nation to reach the moon. I felt tremendous good fortune to be among those selected for this project.

Very little was known about outer space, and nobody knew what perils lurked out there for the crew and vehicle. The goal had already been set: a launch date sometime in the summer of 1969.

Much was accomplished in record time. I marveled at the ingenuity of the technical community in bringing into material form their dreams. I was as enthusiastic about my work as a child on Christmas morning. Throughout the decade of the 1960s I was involved in many fascinating aspects of aerospace— not just the manned space program.

It was a personal victory for me as well as a national triumph when I watched along with an excited world on July 20, 1969, as the astronauts landed on the moon. As America advanced in the space program, I moved forward in my spiritual experience. It seemed as if I were exploring two worlds at the same time. One was outer space with travels to planets and beyond. The other was my inner space with journeys to greater truths and understanding about myself and my relationship with God, meeting new teachers and learning new lessons. The common denominator between these two worlds was the knowledge that both sides enriched my life and gave me an opportunity to see more of God's wonders.

Throughout the 1960s as I worked in aerospace, Doris and I continued with our church membership, prayer groups, and teaching Sunday school. We also started to study the Bible in a more detailed way than we had ever done before. The training from the Navigators paid off. We dug into this study with great interest for we wanted to know everything the Bible had to say to us. This investigation became a *verse by verse* examination of the *entire* Bible.

Doris and I continued to memorize scripture verses so we could fill our minds with the things of God. As we went through the Bible in such detail, we came across many inspiring verses which we wanted to memorize. One was in the book of Isaiah which reaffirmed for me the ever-present guidance of God: "And the Lord shall guide thee continually, and satisfy thy soul in drought, and make fat thy bones: and thou shalt be like a watered garden, and like a spring of water, whose waters fail not." (Isaiah 58:11) This verse has comforted and encouraged me throughout the years. These words helped mold my life, and I noticed how my thinking process changed to harmonize with what I was putting into my mind. Whenever I was faced with difficult circumstances, an appropriate verse would come to mind and help me put things into perspective. I still draw on this method today.

One incident in particular stands out in this regard. Doris and I were having our house painted, and the painter promised to cover all plants and be very careful so that there would be no damage. I was away on a business trip while he painted, and by the time I returned home he had finished and left. When I looked at what he had done, I was aghast. He hadn't put drop cloths on anything, anywhere. Just about everything had paint smears—plants, patio floor, windows, and the lawn. Immediately a verse popped into my mind: "Be ye angry, and sin not . . ." (Ephesians 4:26) It didn't change the situation but it helped me deal with it more calmly.

However, as I moved forward along the spiritual path, I became overconfident and believed that God had entrusted to me the doctrines of faith and truth. I succumbed to my own arrogance and became very dogmatic, a symptom too often experienced by well-meaning but misguided zealots. To some people I had become known as an obnoxious believer, a title I carried with great pride and self-justification.

Usually, in religious discussions I was able to persuade people to my way of thinking, mainly because of my knowledge of the Bible and not necessarily because of a loving manner. As I look back, it is with a certain shame and great remorse. My only defense is that I meant well. I demanded that everyone believe as I believed; otherwise, I assumed that they would most certainly find themselves in an eternal inferno of hell after they died. I sincerely felt as if I were personally responsible for their lives. It took years for me to realize that I carried my concern for them too far.

CHAPTER NINE
ON THE EDGE OF LIGHT

For some time Doris and I had felt a calling to provide a place for youth groups to gather. Such a retreat center could also serve the needs of our missionary friends, a place where they could get away to rest during their furloughs from the mission fields.

Such an opportunity presented itself when we went on vacation in September 1961 to a resort at Big Bear Lake, in the San Bernardino Mountains 120 miles east of Los Angeles. We rented a small cabin and intended to spend a week relaxing and resting. While there, it occurred to us that this might be the area where God would provide the center.

One morning as we studied the Bible, Doris read, "I have given you a land — go in and possess it." (Joshua 1:11) We felt that God was telling us that this indeed was the place.

That very day we contacted a realtor who took us to several cabins that were for sale. None was suitable. Our search continued the next day. While we were in the realtor's office, she told us of a place she thought would be exactly what we were looking for. Unfortunately, as far as she knew, the lady who owned it

wasn't interested in selling. We urged her to call the
owner and ask her if she would be interested. When
the realtor called, the owner asked for what purpose
we wanted it. We explained our hopes for a spiritual
retreat center, and with that explanation the owner
agreed to sell.

The realtor drove us to see the place. It was a large,
rustic lodge called "Midori Land." Immediately, Doris
and I believed this was the "land" about which God
had spoken to us. The property had 300 feet on the
lake, and the lodge was 5,000 square feet of living
space. It seemed to fit all our criteria, and it came completely furnished and set up for retreats. But it was
much larger and more expensive than we had expected. The cost was out of our price range as far as we
were concerned, especially since we still had to live
and work in San Diego. I explained to the realtor that
we needed time to think about it.

For the rest of that vacation week, we spent a great
deal of time in prayer and Bible reading. But when we
returned to San Diego, Doris and I felt disappointed.
We hadn't seen a retreat cabin in our price range, and
it seemed as if God had encouraged us only to let us
down with a hard thump.

A few months later, as I was reading the Bible, I came
across this passage: " . . . How long are ye slack to go
to possess the land, which the Lord God of your fathers hath given you?" (Joshua 18:3) I immediately had
the intuitive sense that this passage was guidance for
me, and I felt embarrassed for having doubted. I
brought up the subject with Doris once again, and
we spent hours examining it from every angle.
What could we do to bring this about? Living in San
Diego and operating a lodge in Big Bear Lake didn't
seem to be within our capabilities. Neither did we con-

sider it reasonable nor wise.

After further discussion we prayed about it—and that prayer changed our direction drastically. I heard myself say aloud to God that, if necessary, I would even sell our home and move up there. Until that moment such an option had never occurred to me. Being a man of my word, I couldn't and wouldn't retract my statement. Doris was a bit shocked to hear such a promise, but she was amenable to do whatever God required of us.

We phoned the realtor in Big Bear Lake and made an offer on the lodge, contingent upon the sale of our home. She presented our offer to the owner, who immediately accepted it.

I quickly put our house on the market, knowing full well that I would have to quit my job if, and when, the house sold.

It was November and the real estate market in our area was stagnant — several homes had been for sale for a number of years with no prospective buyers. That wasn't very encouraging. However, we believed that if it were God's plan for us to have "Midori Land," He would bring us a buyer. That's the way we prayed. If our house didn't sell, we would remain in San Diego, and that was O.K. with us because we loved it there. What we wanted was God's will for us.

Then, early one Sunday morning a month later, as I was reading the Bible, I came across a passage which sprang out at me: ". . . prepare thee stuff for removing and remove by day in their sight; and thou shalt remove from thy place to another place in their sight . . ." (Ezekiel 12:3)

Doris and I both believed that God had given us packing orders to move to Big Bear Lake. We expected that our house would sell *that* day—that He would put

His final approval on our move.

We were at church and away from home all day. As luck would have it, there was a heavy downpour the whole day. We couldn't imagine anyone househunting on a day like that. However, early the next morning at 7 a.m., our realtor called with great news. Our home had sold the day before, having been on the market for less than thirty days.

Now the way was opening up for us. During this period since our vacation at Big Bear Lake, we had used all of our faculties to determine if this move was right. We used our physical energies to contact realtors and to look at properties. We applied our intellectual and emotional energies, trying very hard not to let our own desires distort our spiritual guidance. We had continued our daily spiritual disciplines of praying in the early morning for guidance, reading the Bible, and meditating on the word of God. I was confident that this was God's will and it was the right course for us.

Now I had to give notice to my supervisor at work. He was a very understanding and caring man, and he expressed a sincere interest in my move. I assured him and my fellow engineers that after our move to Big Bear Lake, God would take care of all our needs so I would have no financial worries. Though they showed some interest in what I was telling them, they also didn't believe that all would turn out as rosy as I had described it.

I was overconfident—walking on "cloud nine"—because there was a special feeling about believing that I was in God's perfect will. No discouragement or even caution from others could dampen my spirit. I was happy to be in God's service no matter where it took me.

Doris and I had stationery and brochures printed, and I mailed them to all the churches in southern California in hopes that their youth groups would make reservations for a weekend retreat. I had high hopes and expected overwhelming results.

As the time for moving approached, Doris and I busily packed and said goodbye to the friends we had known for many years. It was hard. I wondered if this move was worth all the emotional pain we were suffering. It was especially difficult to say goodbye to Doris' parents, who were still living in San Diego.

A few days before the moving van was scheduled to arrive, Doris' only brother suddenly began having severe seizures. He was thirty-three years old and lived with his parents. Doris and I spent that whole evening trying to help. We knew that our presence was needed, but we had also made a commitment with God to move to Big Bear Lake. We were torn. Should we cancel the move? Could I get my old job back? This was a difficult time. It was as if the very fiber of our souls was being tried. As much as both of us wanted to stay and help with Doris' brother, we felt we must follow God's guidance. So we proceeded with the move on March 19, 1962.

My faith in God was about to be tested as I stepped out into those unfamiliar mountains and a new life. Settling into our new environment in Big Bear Lake, Doris and I kept ourselves busy working around the lodge from early morning until late at night.

Before moving from San Diego, we had received notice from one church group that they wanted to reserve the retreat center for a weekend. We expected to have the lodge booked with many more church groups in a very short time. But the first week after our arrival no further reservations came in. Undeterred, I was still confident it was only a matter of time before the situation would change for the better.

Before our first group arrived, Doris' brother passed away and she left for San Diego. I was unable to attend the funeral because of my responsibilities at the retreat center. I was all by myself in the lodge, doing the best I could, and it was my first experience being in charge of such a facility. I was nervous. Many times during those three days, I wished that Doris was with me. But overall things went very well with this first group, leaving me eager for our next visitors.

While we waited for more weekend retreat groups, we got involved in the community. One of the first things we did after arriving in Big Bear Lake was to join the Baptist church. The members were in the midst of a building program, so along with other men in the church I helped construct the new sanctuary. It was hard work, but we had fun together. Doris and I faithfully attended the Sunday services and Wednesday evening prayer meetings. Even though I wanted to teach a Sunday school class, I didn't feel I had the time with so much to do at the lodge. Nevertheless, I was sure that someday I would be able to serve in the Sunday School Department. It was something I looked forward to.

Three months passed. Still there were no more retreat center reservations. By then our money had run out, and we were behind in our mortgage payments. Most of our assets had gone toward the down payment on the lodge and the moving costs. I was starting to worry, even though I believed that I had followed God's guidance and was convinced that He would take care of all our needs. Yet, there were no signs of how He planned to do that.

Finally, I knew I had to do something. We were down to our last $20. I had never experienced a financial crisis like this before. There was only one thing to do. I had to find a job—soon.

The following Monday, Doris and I drove back to San Diego. Along the way we reviewed all the guidance we had acted on and tried to understand it better. It was hard to believe that God had led us to the mountaintop only to let us fail. Talking about the predicament, I realized that I was close to losing my faith in God. I was deeply disappointed and completely disillusioned. I had to fight against the feeling of betrayal. But I held steady, remembering the wonderful ways He had worked previously on our behalf.

Doris' parents opened their home to us with loving concern. I called my former employer at General Dynamics and inquired whether or not my old position was still vacant — I wanted to come back to work. My previous supervisor asked me to come in the next day, and shortly thereafter all the arrangements had been made. I was reinstated in my former position at the same salary.

I remember the day I was to report for work—the worst and most humiliating experience I had ever gone through. I walked from the personnel office to my office—very slowly. I hoped the ground would open up and swallow me. I was so ashamed to come back to the same group whom I had told a few months earlier that God would take care of all my needs in the mountains. It was obvious that didn't happen, and I was embarrassed over my failure. This was a very personal disaster, as far as I was concerned. In the few minutes it took to get to my office, I suffered a thousand deaths. What would they say? How would I be received?

As it turned out, my apprehension was unfounded. My former colleagues asked questions about what happened, but they all seemed to understand. I was overwhelmed by their kindness.

Doris and I returned to Big Bear Lake on Friday evening with an unspoken sadness hovering over us. We knew what was about to happen. We were going to be separated for a time. Doris had to stay in the lodge during the week, in case anyone came to look for a retreat facility. I had to be in San Diego to keep my job, and we were going to be together only on weekends. We didn't want to be apart, but what else was there to do?

All during that weekend we talked about possible ways we might have misunderstood the guidance. We considered selling the lodge and returning to San Diego, but we remembered how clear the guidance had been all along. God could have stopped us from buying the property at any point along the way. So we had to follow through, even though things weren't falling into place the way we thought they would.

God couldn't have been the one who made the mistake. It had to have been us. Time and again we went over the steps we had taken in obtaining the guidance and following it. We read and re-read the journal we had kept, yet remained bewildered.

I went back to the basics: God is a good God and wants the best for us. But the same question kept surfacing: Where, how, and why had I failed? The one thing I hadn't wanted to do was to hold down an eight-hour-a-day job while taking care of the retreat center. But now that was exactly the situation in which I found myself. I finally concluded that this was probably where I had misunderstood the guidance. At no time did I get direction from God to quit my job. But in the final analysis, we now had to deal with the reality of our circumstances.

I had earlier traded in our car for a new pickup truck,

anticipating the needs of the lodge. Now I had to drive that truck to get to work in San Diego, leaving Doris stranded at the lodge without transportation. On Sunday afternoon, and many Sunday afternoons thereafter, I made the long drive south. On that lonely trip down the mountains, I worried about how Doris would get to the grocery store, post office, and church. Fortunately, lovely friends from church took her grocery shopping and to the meetings at the church.

My first Sunday evening back in San Diego, I visited the Baptist church where Doris and I had once been members. It just wasn't the same because Doris wasn't with me.

Weekdays I was busy on my job and glad to have it. But my heart was back at Big Bear Lake. I missed Doris and worried about how she was getting along. It wasn't too bad during the day since I had my work to occupy my mind. But the evenings were hard on me. I had the companionship of Doris' parents, but it was a far cry from weekends when Doris and I could be together. Before going to sleep, the last thing I would always say to her was, "I love you," and in the morning these were also the first words I spoke.

As time passed, I started to pursue the possibility of becoming an ordained Baptist minister. I talked with the pastor about it, and he encouraged me to proceed, promising to look into it for me. A few days later he informed me that his inquiries had shown that in order to become ordained it would be necessary to attend a seminary; however, his church could grant me a license to preach, which would be a first step. I would also have to write a comprehensive doctrinal statement on my beliefs. I started on this immediately. My dissertation would eventually be submitted to a panel of ministers and scholars, and I would have to appear before them to defend my positions and answer questions. This board then would make a further determination as to my qualifications.

Several weeks later, at a Sunday evening service, I received my license to preach. In the meantime, I continued to work on my dissertation. I was bogged down because I was unclear about what position to take regarding baptism in the Holy Spirit; therefore, I didn't feel that I was ready to go through an oral examination by a number of pastors and scholars. I delayed submitting my doctrinal statement.

Of course, I had many other items on my mind, too. The lodge in Big Bear Lake and how Doris was doing were frequent concerns for me. Also, I was interested in the charismatic movement. The story of how this interest got started goes back to when Doris and I made several observations of their approach before we moved to Big Bear Lake. At that time we had attended a meeting sponsored by the Full Gospel Businessmen's Fellowship. As advertised, the gathering was held in a very large downtown Presbyterian church. The meeting focused on those who wanted to know more about baptism in the Holy Spirit. At the conclusion of the meeting the speaker invited those who were interested in receiving baptism in the Holy Spirit to come forward and be prayed for. Many people responded. Neither Doris nor I were among them.

This gathering was strange to us. We had been taught, and were teaching, that the gifts of the Spirit were for the early church but not for our time. As a serious Bible student, I was entrenched in the doctrines and statements of faith that I had studied. Consequently it was difficult for me to be open to the possibility of this phenomenon. Neither had I seen any evidence of those gifts in operation in my circle of

Christianity. Nor was I particularly attracted to the speaking in tongues.

Yet there was still something intriguing about these people, even though they didn't appear to be as schooled in the Bible as I was. They had a special spiritual quality about them, their strong points being a genuine love and devotion to Christ.

Our Bible class teacher had told us that speaking in tongues was of the devil, who counterfeited the gift in order to cause confusion and bedlam in the church. We were warned to have nothing to do with it.

Later, we remembered a previous Bible class in which we were taught that the devil counterfeits everything God does. So, at the next Bible class I made a logical point to our teacher: if the devil counterfeits speaking in tongues, then the *real* article must be around some place. I continued by saying that Doris and I were looking for the real thing, not the counterfeit.

Our interest in the charismatics continued after these initial encounters. During our vacation at Big Bear Lake, one item we prayed about was a greater understanding of the baptism in the Holy Spirit. As we read the Bible one day that week, a verse was impressed upon us which seemed to say not to fret over the matter: "For thus saith the Lord, Ye shall not see wind, neither shall ye see rain; yet that valley shall be filled with water, that ye may drink . . . " (II Kings 3:17) This relieved our inner anxiety. We knew then that we would be filled with the Holy Spirit when the time was right for us.

Now to help soften the sting of not having Doris with me, I decided to delve further into the charismatic movement. On weekday evenings I attended several charismatic meetings so that I could observe up close this phenomenon. One evening after such a meeting, I prayed and asked God to help me understand if speaking in tongues was for modern times. If so, I would accept it as a valid doctrine.

Suddenly, in the midst of my prayer, something unusual occurred: I noticed a *foreign word* was interjected into my prayer, something that had never before happened to me. Moments later, there came a second word and then a third. Still, I just kept on praying—in English. My plan was to look up those foreign words later in a concordance or lexicon. But by the time I finished my prayer, I had forgotten the words! I went to sleep with the thought that perhaps something new was beginning to take place within me. The next day at my office I kept thinking about what had happened the night before. It didn't make much sense. What was I to make of it?

I decided to go for a walk around the office building and talk to God. I needed some guidance in evaluating these unusual events. As I walked, I simply asked if the foreign words I had received the night before were from Him or from the devil. Immediately I heard a voice within me say, "Don't call unclean what I have cleansed."

That was my revelation. I was now convinced about the validity of speaking in tongues, and I was eager to share this experience with Doris.

That Friday night I must have flown over the highway in my pickup truck; I was so eager to see Doris and relate to her what had happened. After I had explained my remarkable experience, Doris was as excited about it as I. Even so, it was some time before I pursued it any further. Just dealing with the physical-material challenges in my life at the time was occupying most of my energy.

In the meantime I heard about an engineering firm in San Bernardino with offices at Norton Air Force Base, a short drive from Big Bear Lake. The company needed engineers. As it turned out, it was the same company I had worked for previously in Los Angeles. I applied and within a few weeks I had the job.

Here, I would be working on the Minuteman Missile Program and would monitor contractor compliance with the specifications in various parts of the country. This meant that I'd travel once in a while, but most of the time I'd be in my office.

The trip from my home to Norton was only thirty-four miles, but it took about an hour in good weather over the mountain roads. While driving to and from my office over those lonely roads, I kept my mind occupied. I silently recited scripture passages that I had memorized. I especially enjoyed repeating the epistles of Paul and filling my mind with those teachings.

This exercise helped me to become even better acquainted with God. For two hours each day I was alone with God—no interruptions from any outside source. All was quiet in the cab of my truck as I drove through the scenic parts of the San Bernardino Mountains. I cherished those hours I could spend alone with my God.

About this time the pastor in the Big Bear Lake Baptist Church asked me if I would become Sunday school superintendent. I readily agreed. Since accepting Christ, I had always had a deep desire to serve God, and working in the Sunday School Department was one way to do it. This job was unexpected, and it offered a few unanticipated challenges.

The church bulletin clearly stated that the Sunday School opening exercises started at 9:30 a.m. and classes would begin at 9:45. As Sunday school superintendent, I would be leading the opening exercises in the sanctuary. On the first Sunday, I was there with Doris and the pianist at 9:15 getting things ready. At 9:30 no one had come for the opening exercises. It has always been important to me to have things start on schedule. With only the three of us in the sanctuary, I began the program with a hymn, made a few announcements, and finally led a prayer. I conducted the opening exercises as if the whole sanctuary was filled to capacity. At 9:45 I dismissed the three of us for Sunday school.

A few minutes later people started to straggle in, and I told them to proceed to their classes so they wouldn't be too late. Apparently the members of the church didn't think anything would start on time, so they paid no attention to the schedule.

The following Sunday morning it was a little better—a few people came in time for my opening. The third week everyone who attended Sunday school was present at 9:30.

During the opening exercises, I taught the small children scripture songs. A favorite of mine is based on Psalm 89, and one Sunday morning I taught it to the children. "We will sing of the mercies of the Lord . . ." The following Wednesday night at the prayer meeting, I met the parents of one of the little boys in Sunday school. They remarked how much their son liked the scripture songs I was teaching. The father laughed and told me that last week his son had come home from Sunday school singing, "Ve Vill sing of the mercies of the Lord forever . . . " He asked his son if Aron had taught him a new song that morning, the father recognizing how he had picked up my Norwegian accent.

My involvement with this little church became more

and more time consuming, but it helped me grow spiritually. I initiated a training program for Sunday school teachers, believing that anything worth doing was worth doing right and well. Doris and I sang in the choir; I was appointed deacon, later elected head deacon.

By now our lodge retreat center was receiving a number of reservations for youth groups, and soon we were completely booked for the coming winter season. Groups were scheduled from many different denominations. Frankly, I was a little suspicious of them and their beliefs. For the most part I had been around only fundamentalists.

In my church circles I thought I could always tell if anyone truly knew God by the words and phrases they used to express their religious beliefs. If they didn't use the right words and phrases in the right places, I became suspicious that perhaps they hadn't really experienced a personal relationship with Christ like I had. Conformity was an important factor in my religious quest at that time.

But that winter as I talked to these guests—Episcopalians, Lutherans, Methodists, and many others—I discovered that even though they didn't use my phraseology, they had a deep and meaningful commitment to Christ. That surprised me. It wasn't easy at first for me to accept the fact that there were others besides fundamentalists who knew God on a personal level.

When the lodge was filled with youngsters on retreat, Doris and I were so busy we didn't have time for each other. The only private moments we had were when we took the garbage to the dump on Sunday afternoons after the groups had left. We began to look forward to our "romantic" trips to the dump. Upon returning from the dump, I scrubbed out the garbage cans with hot water and soap. To some extent the groups cleaned up after themselves, but during the week while I was at work, Doris always had to prepare the lodge, scrubbing and sanitizing the bathrooms, dusting and vacuuming to make the place presentable for the next group. It was our belief that all of this cleaning was as spiritual as praying for the sick or preaching from the pulpit. We felt we were serving God by making the lodge available to church groups.

On weekends when we had groups at the lodge, I played over the loudspeaker system recordings of instrumental music that was inspirational and quieting. After several years of keeping the same tape recorder in good repair, it finally gave up the ghost, creating an immediate need to find a replacement. We had no money for one, but that didn't stop me from looking.

On my weekday lunch hours I went to stores where such equipment was sold, conducting a thorough investigation to find the best equipment for our needs. Though money was in very short supply, I knew my God was rich. Therefore, I looked for a quality recorder which would perform well under constant use and have the features we needed, such as automatic tape reversal to provide continuous music without my having to attend it.

In a discount store I found a recorder which would fill the need, but the price was very high. In 1965, $350 for a tape recorder was very expensive. But I remembered the biblical truth that my God owned the cattle on a thousand hills, including the hills. So I decided that this recorder was the one we should have. I got a brochure on the equipment and took it home to show Doris.

We prayed very earnestly for this tape recorder and

thanked God for it. Then we placed the brochure on the wall in our bedroom, and whenever we saw it we would say, "Thank You, Father." We learned also to say, "This or better."

God did indeed answer our prayers. Two weeks later we received a donation for $200. A few days after that someone else gave us $100, and a third person donated $25.00. They didn't know that we needed a tape recorder, so we were thrilled to see how God provided for our need. With an additional $25.00 of our own funds, we had the new tape recorder.

Many years later we were surprised to find a book called *Treasure Mapping* in a Unity bookstore. Its principles are the same we used to get our tape recorder, but this book deals with the subject in a very comprehensive, positive, and detailed way.

One day I learned from my pastor that a new revised version of the Bible had been released. I borrowed his copy and compared a number of its sections with those from the King James version and other translations. In each case I found that this new translation differed with my findings of what the original Hebrew meant for the passages in question. I made my discovery known to the pastor. He told me that a delegation from the Baptist seminary would soon give a presentation of this new translation at a meeting in our church.

Of course, Doris and I were present on the evening of that presentation. I listened to the talk with undivided attention. When it came to the portions of the Bible which I felt had been mistranslated, I asked the Bible scholar in charge of this forum why such changes had been made. He answered that in order to understand the real meaning of those passages I had to know Hebrew. Then he asked, "You don't know Hebrew, do you?" I told him that I could read Hebrew fluently and invited him to go on with his explanation. Instead, he claimed that it would take too much time and, besides, they had to close the meeting.

I had hoped to have an answer to my question. But it made me feel proud that I had been able to wrestle with a scholar and win. Looking back, I know I might have been a bit too arrogant. Yet I had done it for the sole purpose of finding an answer on the subject, not to humiliate him. When I think of my attitude at that time, I'm embarrassed because I wanted to set everybody straight. Since then I've learned better.

CHAPTER TEN

FIRST GLIMPSES
OF A DEEPER MINISTRY

Our pastor, who knew of my desire to become an ordained minister in the Baptist denomination, on his own volition contacted the dean of a large Baptist seminary. He inquired about the possibility of a correspondence course for me which might lead to a seminary degree. The reply, which he showed me, was not encouraging. There were no correspondence courses available. I thanked him for his concern and told him it was very thoughtful of him to take the time to write on my behalf.

Since ordained ministry seemed out of my reach, I looked to find my calling in another way. I had often heard Bible teachers and pastors urge Christians to "find their ministry" in the church, and I thought I had found mine—teaching Sunday school. But friends in my church kept encouraging me to look for something more—to keep trying to find my true ministry. Their comments troubled and concerned me because I didn't know where to look.

That concern opened a new door, taking me to another plateau in my spiritual growth. One day when I was alone in the kitchen of our home in Big Bear Lake, this concern was still on my mind. Just then I heard a voice speak to me! It was as clear as if someone else were in the room. I looked around to see if, by chance, someone had slipped into the kitchen, only to discover that I was still alone. This is what the voice said: "You have no ministry. But if you would allow Me, I can minister everything through you." In other words, He was telling me that He was the Giver of all things, and, as such, He could minister anything and everything through me. I immediately understood and believed the voice to be that of Jesus Christ.

In the quietness of the moments that followed, I thought of the words He had spoken, and it made sense. He could have said, "Why limit yourself in one particular ministry; why sell yourself short when you can have it all, provided you are willing to let Me work through you?"

I have vividly remembered that experience and taken it to heart.

In spite of the spiritually powerful boost that experience gave me, there was still the unresolved issue of the gifts of the Spirit which I had laid aside for some time. Soon I had to face it again and had to deal with it.

One Friday night I came home late. I had been on the East Coast all week on business and was tired. I looked forward to seeing Doris, but she wasn't home. That was very unusual, and I wondered where she could be. I called a friend who I thought would know. Sure enough, Doris was there attending a prayer meeting. At eleven o'clock at night? I informed Doris in no uncertain terms that she was to come home—now.

Before long she arrived. I was furious. I wanted to know what she was doing out so late. What I found out shocked and enraged me. Doris hadn't put aside the matter of seeking the gifts of the Spirit, as I had. Every night that week she had gone to the same Holy Spirit prayer meeting. Some friends from the Baptist church were attending these meetings and having wonderful experiences with the baptism in the Holy Spirit. Doris explained that she would have been home by 9 p.m. that night, but this had been a glorious meeting. Our close friends, an older couple, had received the baptism. A spirit of joy and laughter had come upon everyone present. Doris and the others had lost all track of time, she said.

"I don't know about all this," I complained angrily, simultaneously remembering my own experience when unknown words had come to me. "I got only three words. How can that be a language?"

Despite my rage, Doris was very patient with me. She suggested soothingly that simply because I didn't receive a complete language was no reason for me to be angry. She reminded me that when people apply what they know, usually more knowledge comes. I could apply that principle to this very subject.

She recommended, "Use those three words during your prayer time. Repeat them several times. Give it a chance. I'm sure more words will come."

Unfortunately, I had forgotten those three words. Perhaps, it was too late. But Doris encouraged me with specific words of instruction she had recently learned. I should present myself again to God in prayer, asking the Lord Jesus to baptize me. Next I was to relax and have a time of thanksgiving, praise, and love for God. Then, if and when strange words came, I should let them come and use them as I continued in prayer. She reminded me that I hadn't been very open to speaking in tongues and that attitude may have set up a mental block.

As I calmed down, I had to admit that she was right. Now I had come to grips with the matter and finally agreed that the gift of tongues—along with the other gifts of the Spirit—were indeed for our modern times. So, I would try again and this time be as open as I could to all that the Holy Spirit had for me. Afterward in my prayer time more and more words came. Finally, as far as this matter was concerned, I was at peace with myself and God.

Doris had dragged me kicking and screaming into the charismatic movement, and I am thankful that she did. It brought a new dimension of Christ to my awareness. It was as if Jesus appeared in a new light and was a closer presence. I became enthused all over again, just as when I met Christ in my dream years previously. We found that as we "prayed in the Spirit" (as we called it) there was such a feeling of love and peace filling our inner beings.

Doris and I moved into this new phase with fervor. Upon restudying the scripture passages pertaining to the gifts of the Spirit, we decided to accept the teaching at face value. We began to have a better understanding and saw them manifested in our home prayer meetings. Between the two of us, we saw much of God's wonders and miracles. Among them was the gift of prophecy, followed by the word of knowledge and wisdom, as explained in I Corinthians, Chapters 12 through 14. This always amazed both of us.

There was much more to knowing God than we had thought. His presence became an even greater reality than before. I started to experience a closer, deeper, and more meaningful relationship with God than I had thought possible.

God started using Doris and me in a very dramatic fashion to help others. What followed was the seed of something that later blossomed into my ability to give psychic readings to help thousands of individuals. But the beginnings were directly out of my experiences in the charismatic movement.

During these times Doris became very sensitive to moments when the Spirit wished to give a message through me to a group. I wasn't always alert to the Spirit's prompting, but she would get my attention so I could quiet myself and then a message would come.

On one occasion after Bible study in a friend's home, we were all standing around having refreshments and visiting. I was talking with some of the men, and Doris was talking with some of the women when she began to feel the presence of the Spirit for a message. She told me later how she had waited a bit, watching me to see if I were alert to it. Since I showed no evidence of being aware, Doris thought that she had better get my attention.

She slipped up quietly behind me and whispered that the Spirit wanted my attention. I quieted myself to see if I felt it, too. Immediately I was alerted to His presence. I alerted the others in the room, saying that I felt that God had a message for us and asked if we could all quiet ourselves. I closed my eyes and offered myself to God and asked if He wished to speak. In a moment words began coming to me and I spoke them aloud: "My children, your seeking after Me in these studies brings Me great pleasure. I send My blessings on you for your continued spiritual growth."

Two of the couples exclaimed that they had just been discussing how busy they were and how difficult it was to find time to attend these Bible studies. They had been wondering if they should continue. They were convinced by those words that their attendance was pleasing to God. Knowing this, there was no way that they would stop coming.

But these new developments weren't pleasing to everyone. Our Baptist minister heard that we were newly involved with the baptism in the Holy Spirit. He asked Doris and me, along with three other couples, to meet with him after the Sunday evening service. He sat down with the eight of us and began scolding us for involving ourselves in something that wasn't accepted Baptist doctrine. He sternly warned us to stop. Furthermore, he forbade us to go to any other church for any meetings or to gather in each others' homes for such meetings.

We all were somewhat stunned. After a moment I spoke. I reminded him that whenever our church doors were open, we were there. But when there were no meetings in our church, Doris and I felt free to attend other churches or prayer meetings we might choose. This suggestion infuriated him. That's when he proclaimed his ultimatum: We must recant the experience with the baptism in the Holy Spirit or else leave the church.

For Doris and me the solution was clear. I looked at Doris and she smiled. Turning to the pastor, I explained that we couldn't deny our experience with God. Our friends agreed. If it meant leaving the church, we would leave.

He leaned back into his chair and shook his head. "I just don't understand it," he said. "My best people! Choir director, organist, deacons, Sunday school teachers."

Then someone spoke calmly. It was the organist. "Pastor," she said, "that should tell you something."

But he didn't get the message.

So we left the church. At the time it was very painful, but in retrospect I can see the irony in what happened. Years earlier when we were received into this Baptist church as members we were given, as is commonly known, the right hand of fellowship. Suddenly we were being told to leave, and we were getting the left foot of fellowship. We were kicked out.

The people in the Baptist church were wonderful friends, and we loved them and they us. It was very painful for us to leave. But we believed then, and still do today, that it was a sacrifice we were forced to make if we were to maintain our spiritual convictions. After that we attended a small assembly where the gifts of the Spirit were being exercised. The other three couples, Doris, and I all felt free to worship there.

I also joined the Full Gospel Businessmen's Fellowship and eventually became one of the vice presidents in the local chapter. This proved to be a further means of service to God. The leaders of the chapter were very supportive and encouraged me in my spiritual growth. My faith and confidence grew as I matured in the operation of the gifts. Confidence also revealed itself in such mundane matters as obtaining inspirational speakers for the monthly dinner meetings to which our wives were also invited.

From time to time many chapters joined together for a large rally. This gave me opportunities to hear and meet a number of internationally known men of God. They inspired me to trust God in a greater measure as they shared from their own experiences.

One such speaker was a world leader in the charismatic movement. For months I had tried to engage him as a speaker for our chapter. However, each time I phoned his office he was out of town or out of the country.

Sometime later, I had to be in Boston on business for my company, and I remembered a well-known conference center in New Hampshire. I telephoned the owner to see if she knew of any top speakers who soon might be out on the West Coast and be willing to speak to our chapter. She replied that Dr. Ravin was at her center speaking that week. Perhaps he would know of someone. As it happened, he was the world leader I had been trying to contact for several months.

"Do you suppose I could come and have a word with him?" I asked. She gave me directions from Boston. It would be about a two-hour drive. I would get there just in time for dinner. So, I rented a car and I was on my way at 5 p.m.

The owner had graciously arranged for me to sit across the table from Dr. Ravin at dinner. He was a man of slight build, snow white hair, and wore glasses. He impressed me as a very gentle man, and he spoke with a fine English accent. I got right down to business. "Will you speak at our chapter, and can you right now give me a date for it?"

He pulled out his appointment book and said, "If you went to the trouble to come all the way up here from Boston to get me to speak to your chapter, how can I turn you down? I'll put you in my schedule for next month."

I was back at my hotel by 11 p.m. and called my chapter president. He was ecstatic to have a person of Dr. Ravin's stature as our speaker and promised to get the word out right away to the members. My confidence enabled me to go to any lengths possible to obtain speakers of great substance for our chapter. Those times were periods of great growth for me. I had lost the fellowship of my church at Big Bear Lake, but had found other avenues to serve my God.

God rewarded me with an ever-increasing base of knowledge and understanding, especially in regard to yet another gift of the Spirit: healing. Naturally I hoped that this would be prominent in my ministry. As Doris and I prayed for the sick, sometimes we saw results, but there were times when nothing happened. I didn't understand why some were healed and others weren't. But undeterred, I kept praying whenever someone requested it.

I wanted to know as much about this miracle of healing as I could. Doris and I read many books about the subject. Being trained as an engineer, I tried to analyze how healing took place—why it happened and what was the mechanism. Soon I gave up. I couldn't find a technique that worked the same way every time. Naively, I expected to discover a fool-proof recipe for healing prayer. But mysterious factors just beyond my level of faith seemed to play a role in successful healings.

About this time a difficult test occurred, demanding all my attention and patience. Doris developed muscle spasms over her entire back. For days she was in bed. She could barely walk; and when she did, it was with great pain. It didn't get any better, and I was beside myself, not knowing what to do.

One Saturday morning around 3 a.m. Doris woke me. She told me that the pain was very severe and asked if I would please do something. I got up, went to her side of the bed, and prayed for her. The pain remained. Then I sat by the bed in a chair and read the Bible to her, hoping that perhaps something in the scripture might serve as a catalyst for her healing. At 6 a.m. the pain continued, from time to time even seeming to get worse. Lovingly, I suggested perhaps it might help to soak in a hot tub of water. With great effort I moved her. Thirty minutes later I helped her back into bed. The pain hadn't diminished. I had exhausted every course I could think of to ease her pain and was deeply discouraged that my efforts hadn't helped.

Later, I made breakfast for the two of us. While she ate, she supported herself as best she could with her elbows on the table. I could see the excruciating pain in her eyes, and I could almost feel it myself. It was a heart-rending sight. I was at the end of my rope. What could I do to bring her some relief? Everything I had done was useless.

In desperation and compassion, I took Doris' hands in mine. Quietly, I pleaded with God to heal her *NOW*. Then something happened. Immediately Doris sat up straight. Tears came to her eyes. She exclaimed that every pain had left her body as I had said *"NOW."* No evidence of pain was left. We were so elated that with tears streaming down our faces, we hugged and thanked our God for the healing.

The pain was really gone. As evidence, right after breakfast Doris helped me move a double bed mattress and box springs to another part of the lodge— something she'd never have been able to do a couple of hours earlier.

I had discovered that healing prayer doesn't have to be long nor flowery. I'll probably never know why my other efforts to help failed, but I do know that my short, sincere prayer for Doris' healing worked. To this day I'm still amazed that it happened the way it did. I'd never seen anything as dramatic as that take place before my eyes. Stepping-stones such as this incident have sharpened our insight. They have taught us to be alert to the many ways God chooses to guide and heal us in our daily lives.

In our life at the lodge, we had settled into a routine. I still did some traveling, and many weekends we had retreat groups as our guests. The new tape recorder functioned very well. I was able, with some occasional help, to maintain the lodge upkeep, and every summer

I had time to split five cords of wood to fuel the two fireplaces during the upcoming winter. It was hard, physical work, and I enjoyed it.

By fall the property taxes on the lodge were coming due. Our income hadn't allowed us to put money aside from our own resources. I didn't want to borrow money from my credit union at work, although that was an option. I felt that there must be another way. I prayed about it for several weeks. Nothing happened.

One afternoon while I was praying about the need for tax money, the phone rang. It was a realtor who told me that a vacant lot Doris and I had offered for sale some time ago had finally sold. I could pick up the check in a few days. To my surprise, the amount of the check was enough to cover the tax bill—almost to the penny. This was another in a growing list of episodes where God worked on our behalf.

I shared stories such as this one when asked to speak before charismatic groups. I was often called upon to speak by charismatic leaders both because of my conversion experience from Judaism to Christianity and a growing awareness by others of my trust in God's guidance. I continually left myself open for new opportunities to serve like this.

At one of the meetings I met a man who asked if I could record on tape the New Testament in Hebrew. He wanted to reproduce the tapes and give them to people in Israel who might want them. I told him I wasn't sure if I could do it, but I would like to try. I couldn't promise anything. Evidently he had faith that I could do it because he supplied me with a tape recorder and an editing machine. Nobody in his office knew Hebrew, he said, so I had to do my own editing. It became a challenge that I struggled with for a long time. This was a tedious process and took a great deal of my time. I thought I could have the entire New Testament finished in six months, but I was wrong.

I wanted to serve God and believed this translation task and the speaking engagements offered me that opportunity. While I wasn't complacent, nevertheless I became quite comfortable with my spiritual growth, and I was eager to share my testimony with those who were interested. God had taken me a step at a time to new plateaus, but the one that came next startled me and led me along a whole new path. Little did I realize how all the events up until now were simply a preparation for a type of service I'd never imagined.

As I spoke in front of Full Gospel and charismatic groups, God began to give me a word of prophecy for individuals in the audience. Obviously, this turn of events surprised them—and me, too. Previously I had sometimes given prophetic messages that were for any and all to hear. But what began to come through me now was always personally pertinent to a single individual. These messages were always for people I had never met before!

For example, at a meeting in the Los Angeles area, just as I was ready to conclude my lecture, a message came through me for a young man who was sitting in the front row: "God has called you to serve Him, and it will not be on this continent."

As soon as the meeting concluded, the young man came over to me and said that the message confirmed what he himself had felt led to do. He was scheduled to go to the Philippines, and this personal message helped him to know that he was making the right decision.

On another occasion, I was invited to speak to a group in Santa Maria. During my talk, a message from God was directed to a man seated in the rear of the room. I announced to him that God had a message for him, but I wanted to give it to him privately, and I asked him to see me after the meeting. Later, after nearly everyone had gone, he came up to me. I said to him, "God is very displeased because you've been running away from Him." The man confirmed that the message was most certainly for him. He told me that he lived in Los Angeles, but had been running from God for some time. He happened to be in Santa Maria and heard of this meeting. He was hoping that he would hear something that would release him from a promise he had made to God. Instead, the message reinforced the fact that he had to fulfill it. With that, he pledged to give up his resistance, stop running, and keep his promise. I didn't question him about the situation; I just let him tell me as much as he wanted me to know.

These prophetic messages began to happen so frequently that word got around that I could get information from God for individuals. People began calling and writing to me for a message from God. With Doris' assistance, we always complied.

In the meantime, I received a new assignment on my job. An important test program was to be conducted in the field, and I was asked to go on temporary relocation to Waltham, a suburb west of Boston. I was to be in charge of the program. A friend of ours agreed to take care of things for us at the lodge, allowing Doris to accompany me. Before starting the assignment, I flew to Waltham to look for an apartment. The only affordable option available for just a few months was a motel room with kitchen facilities. Unfortunately, it was a long distance from my new office, and this was especially problematic since I had to be on call twenty-four hours a day, seven days a week for the duration of the test program. On my way back to my office, I had a talk with God. I told Him that I knew He must have something better than that for Doris and me. All the way back I kept talking aloud to God—fortunately, the car windows were closed and nobody heard me as I drove through the streets.

When I got back to my office, I found some encouraging news. An engineer who had been to the personnel office had seen a sign on the bulletin board advertising a nearby apartment for rent. He knew that I was looking for housing so he took the card and gave it to me as soon as I returned.

Immediately I drove to the apartment and found it suitable. It was furnished with dishes, pots, and pans. I rented it on the spot. The apartment was located within walking distance of the office.

I knew that God had answered my prayer even while I was talking to Him. As has so often happened throughout my life of requesting and receiving guidance, what He provided was much better than what I could find on my own.

Doris and I stayed there for almost two months, and during that time Doris' father passed away. The next day she was on her way to California for the funeral, and for the following week I was all alone. I missed her very much and counted the hours until she got back.

When this phase of the test program was finished, we drove from Waltham to Grand Forks, North Dakota, where the last part of the test program was to take place. This phase took two weeks; and when it was finished, Doris and I were on our way back to California.

All along the way, going out east and now coming back west, I knew that God was leading us in a very sure way. Like so many times in the past, my concerns and worries over the details of material life had been resolved generously, and I was so thankful for His provisions. It was comforting to be in His will and to be heading back home to Big Bear Lake. Little did I realize what lay just ahead as new spiritual challenges were on the horizon.

CHAPTER ELEVEN
THE SEEMINGLY OBVIOUS

U pon returning to Big Bear Lake, we began to have weekly charismatic meetings in our home. After one such meeting, while I was talking to someone, I noticed that a friend put a pamphlet on the dining room table and walked away. I took that to mean that he wanted me to read it, but he didn't want to engage me in a debate about the subject. He knew how well versed I was in the Bible and anything pertaining to it. So he apparently thought it wiser to let me read the pamphlet by myself.

As soon as our guests left, I picked up the pamphlet, curious to read it. As soon as I started to read, the concepts stopped me in my tracks. It was asking me to re-evaluate my understanding of one of the strongest doctrines of fundamental Christian theology—the question of how far God's mercy would extend. I was standing at a spiritual crossroads.

The pamphlet was entitled "The Outcome of Infinite Grace," by Dr. Loyal F. Hurley. I leafed through the pages, but initially I quickly discounted it. However, to satisfy my curiosity, I picked it up again soon thereafter and read further.

Every page brought righteous indignation. The author was wrong! His conclusions conflicted with all my Baptist training. After all, I knew the truth, I thought. This poor, misguided fellow obviously didn't understand the scriptures.

Haughtily, I told Doris that his doctrine opposed God's will. Time and again, the author suggested that *all* people would finally see God—that there was no eternal hell and that God would have mercy on everyone. Finally, I became so enraged that I threw the booklet across the room. In those days I wasn't known to have patience for views that conflicted with my own.

However, Doris picked it up and started to read. She was more rational than I. After finishing it, she surprised me by stating that there was ample scripture presented to support his premise. Doris' comments caused me to reconsider. She suggested that the subject warranted further study.

I reluctantly agreed—not because I believed there was any truth to that teaching, but because I assumed that by studying its concepts I could prove the author wrong. I had proven people wrong before—Bible teachers and scholars alike. This shouldn't be any different, I thought. We decided to read the booklet once through together first before going back and studying it more carefully.

When we finished it for the second time, I still wanted to forget it. But Doris suggested that we study the Bible verses he used to validate his claim so that we could draw our own conclusions.

Painfully, I agreed to do the research. Little did I realize what I was in for. Although I wanted to prove this author wrong, still I wanted to be honest and actually seek the truth of the matter. I already knew that famous scholars agreed on an eternal hell for all who didn't accept Jesus Christ as their savior. But I needed to follow through on their references to see if the scriptures actually confirmed what they taught. For the moment, I had to be objective and negate my personal opinions so that I could be open to the truth.

By this time in my spiritual growth, I recognized that I still had a lot to learn; I didn't know all of the plan and purpose of God. Over and over again I had been shown that God has a way of revealing a greater truth than first meets the eye. Just a few items were required of me: a determination to seek the truth, a little curiosity, and some flexibility and willingness to change my direction if needed.

Unfortunately, it was very difficult to let go of my "truth" and security. But I had promised Doris that I would make an unbiased, sincere study of this question of just how far God's mercies extended. So I began by plunging into this investigation with a vengeance.

It has been said that there is an attitude that blocks all information, renders all arguments invalid, and guarantees to keep a person in eternal ignorance. That attitude is spiteful investigation. I'll have to admit that I certainly entered this study with a heavy measure of contempt. Yet, I desired truth, so I reduced my contempt to curiosity, believing I could prove Dr. Hurley wrong.

With the academic training I had received in the field of science, I considered myself to have a scientific spirit. But this scriptural investigation made me wonder, What exactly is the scientific spirit?

I was reminded of the words of Dr. David L. Cooper, in his book *Messiah: His First Coming Scheduled*: "What is the scientific spirit? Several things: first, an open mind; second, readiness to gather all the facts whatever the cost; third, an impartial examination of all evidence and data with a view of determining the truth, the whole truth, and nothing but the truth; and finally, courage to discard whatever is found to be untrue, to accept the newly discovered facts, and to act accordingly."

Each evening after work, I hurried up the mountain to Big Bear Lake to continue my search in the scriptures. Dinner over with, I got out all my reference books—the Hebrew Bible, the interlinear Greek Bible, the English New Testament, plus several other versions of the Bible, a concordance, the Hebrew and Greek lexicons, and whatever else I might need.

In essence, this pamphlet asserted the infinite grace of God, presenting the premise that everyone will eventually come to know the Creator. It introduced a section of scripture references for each of three opposing doctrinal statements: one, eternal torment; two, extermination; and three, reconciliation with God. Each section in itself was convincing and gave many scripture passages that clearly confirmed the point for that respective belief. This could cause legitimate confusion, I thought. But the author went on to explain that once a person understands the biblical usage of certain words, much of the seemingly contradictory precepts in the Bible would be cleared up.

For instance, he asked: "How long is eternal? Everlasting and forever?" Dr. Hurley pointed out that in biblical usage these words often occur in passages where it can't possibly mean unending. Take the story from the Old Testament in which a servant desired to stay with his master. The master took an awl and pierced his ear, saying he would be his servant "forever." (Deuteronomy 15:16-17) The time served lasted only for his lifetime and *not* forever, in the sense of an unending period of time.

I researched diligently the words "eternal" and "everlasting" and "forever," beginning with their usage in the Old Testament. This required four hours of study every evening for the next three weeks.

After forty pages of notes and all those hours, I gave up. Reluctantly, I had to admit that Dr. Hurley was right. I shared with Doris my findings and my chagrin at having taught so dogmatically the doctrine of eternal hell. This was devastating for me. I would have to make quite a departure from my old ways of thinking and teaching in order to bring out the truth as I could now see it.

This intellectual change, in turn, had a profound effect on other parts of my life in the days ahead. I began to experience a great love for all people. I started seeing them as my brothers and sisters, regardless of what they did or didn't believe. To me this was quite a revelation. The truth of the matter was now obvious to me. Unfortunately, it hadn't been so obvious at the beginning of my search.

It is embarrassing to admit that I had been wrong about anything, but especially something as important as spiritual teachings. But how much worse it would have been to continue in the wrong precept once I knew the truth about it. I determined I'd rather follow the truth no matter what the cost.

Of course, this wasn't the first time that I was forced to reevaluate a belief that I had previously embraced in a wholehearted way. Having been raised in an Orthodox Jewish home in Norway, I hadn't begun my spiritual search until after coming to the United States. The dream experience with Jesus Christ demanded that I adopt a whole new world view. At that time I studied hard to obtain a scriptural background for my new belief and for my Christian experience.

Sometimes there is a high price to pay for following the truth. Often it means going in a different direction

from friends and family members. In my case, important people from early in my life ended up discarding
me, believing that I had embraced an unsound philosophy. Following the truth *as I knew it* led to being
misunderstood and to feelings of rejection, such as
when we were asked to leave the Baptist church. But I
have always found that a total dedication to the search
for truth is worth any sacrifice.

The confrontation with Dr. Hurley's little pamphlet
had truly been a spiritual crossroads for me. Now it
became inconceivable to Doris and me that a loving
God would have a plan to send any of His creation to
an eternal hell. I know that I would have little respect
for a father whose last will and testament declared
that, if any of his children didn't do this or that, the
result would be for them to suffer in an eternal hell
forever. If this kind of will were made public, there
would be an outcry of indignation against such a cruel
father.

Yet, for centuries religions of the Western world have
depicted God as that kind of a cruel father. My closer
study of the scriptures gave me a broader view so I
could accept that His grace toward humanity is in-
credibly infinite.

I learned to remind myself in all my studies that
God is neither a Baptist nor a Presbyterian, nor any
other denomination. God was and is God.

Not long after having changed my mind about the
doctrine of eternal hell, I approached yet another cross-
road along my path of spiritual enlightenment. I was
about to be introduced to the life of Edgar Cayce.

In 1965, after another charismatic meeting in our
home, a new challenge was introduced by the wife of a
Presbyterian minister. She and her husband had said
their goodbyes and were headed for the door when she

turned and asked the question, "Have you read anything about Edgar Cayce?" I told her I hadn't. "You
must read a book called *There Is a River* by Thomas
Sugrue," she urged. I asked what the story was about.
She replied simply that if this book didn't bring me
closer to God, forget the book and forget Edgar Cayce.

My time was precious; I didn't like to waste it — especially by reading material that didn't teach me
anything. I wanted a synopsis of the book to make sure
that reading it wouldn't be a waste of time. Yet, I was
intrigued by her challenge that this book could bring
me closer to God. I've always liked challenges. I'm open
to anything that can help me get closer to God.

I immediately bought the book and began reading it.
In retrospect, I can see what a tremendous soul-
searching was sparked in me by this man's life. I found
that Edgar Cayce was a man after my own heart. He
had a personal relationship with God. So did I. He read
the Bible every day, and he taught a Sunday school
class in his church. So did I. On these very important
features, our lives seemed identical. If I hadn't seen
those spiritual credentials, I would have been leery of
reading on or trusting the validity of what transpired
in his life.

Then I came to a part of the book that was a real
problem for me. Cayce had come to believe in a concept called reincarnation. I began to wonder, Could
reincarnation really be in the plan of God? I became
deeply concerned. What if it were? Here was Edgar
Cayce, a man devoted to God, who struggled hard with
the idea and finally came to accept it. Perhaps I should
study this thoroughly.

Not surprisingly, the concept of reincarnation was
not easy for me to embrace. It was foreign to the teachings of the Christian faith, as I understood them. At

least I hadn't come across anything about it or recognized it in my studies up to that time. Frankly, I hadn't even given it any thought.

But now my question wasn't why others believed or had not believed in reincarnation. Instead, here was the question I focused on: Is this part of God's teaching and purpose for humanity? In the final analysis, it's unimportant to me whether or not others believe in this concept. If it's part of God's truth, I want to know it. Those were the guidelines that directed my intense study of the Bible now. I had to know, first of all, if there was a basis for it in the scriptures.

I remembered from my studies that Jesus told His disciples that John the Baptist was Elijah. (Matthew 17:10-13) Previously I hadn't been open to the possibility that Jesus was indicating that John the Baptist was the reincarnated Elijah. Then, I thought about the scriptural story in which the disciples asked the Master about the man born blind. (John 9:1-3) Was he blind because he had sinned? But *when* could he have sinned? I was perplexed. It would have had to have been before he was born into this life. For the disciples to have asked such a question, belief in previous lives must have been common, I reasoned. Otherwise, Jesus would have corrected them. I read and re-read these Bible verses. I looked for further scriptural evidence, one way or the other. While I was struggling with these questions, I had a vivid experience.

I dreamed that I was on the East Coast, in the area around Boston, during the time of the Puritans. I noticed that my clothing was identical to that which the people wore at that time. I saw a man whom I knew to be my father, although he was not the same as my father in this present life. Yet, the whole episode was very real to me, and I knew right then and there that this was a life where I had been on earth.

When I woke up, the entire dream seemed to have been a replay of what had taken place in a previous life. I could still feel profoundly the reality of that lifetime as it appeared in the dream. This experience was a strong confirmation to me that what I was studying about reincarnation was valid.

Sometime later, while we had a group in our lodge for the weekend, I felt the need to get off by myself. I went to our bedroom and stretched out across the bed. All that day and for many days previously I had been thinking about the issue of reincarnation. I prayed for a while, asking God to speak to me about all this. I closed my eyes, thinking I might take a nap, but I didn't go to sleep. Instead I had a vision.

I was standing on the seashore, wading in water ankle-deep. I heard the breakers crashing against the shore with a tremendous force. About where the waves crashed, I noticed a number of jagged rocks protruding above the surface of the water. As I looked beyond the breakers, the water was very quiet and I could see several people swimming. All of them beckoned to me to come out and join them. But fear overtook me, and I backed away from the water.

No sooner had I done so than I felt two strong hands on my back, near my shoulders, and I was pushed into the water. I swam through the breakers and joined the others who were out in the deep water. One swimmer in the group told me that, if I had stayed just off the shore and played in that area, I soon would have been caught by the breakers, tossed against the rocks, and injured. I understood immediately that I was safer in the deep water. Then the visionary experience ended.

I opened my eyes and thought about what had been revealed to me. A verse from the Gospel of Luke came to me: "Launch out into the deep, and let down your nets for a draught." (Luke 5:4)

In a part of my mind, I had been thinking of reincarnation as "going off the deep end." But the message was guiding me to launch out into that deep water where there would be much to learn. Twice now God had shown me in my own inner experiences that reincarnation was real and that it was something I should embrace. I got up from my bed feeling very refreshed. My worries and concerns about the validity of reincarnation were gone. I knew I could accept it as truth.

I saw the wisdom and mercy of God in it. The concept that I had lived before and, no doubt, would live again had now become part of my understanding.

As for Edgar Cayce, I was impressed by his life and his work. He was a dedicated Christian and had a most unusual and unorthodox ministry. As a young man, he discovered somewhat by accident that he could spontaneously put himself into a trance-like altered state of consciousness. From this unusual level of awareness, he seemed to be able to tap into universal knowledge. He was able to answer accurately almost any kind of question put to him. He could get information for healing those who were ill and who suffered from physical and spiritual conflicts.

I wished that I could have known Cayce personally. But it was too late. Edgar Cayce had died in 1945. Yet, the story of his life has had a significant impact on my growth and opened doors to spiritual concepts that completely redirected and changed my life. Little did I realize at the time that Cayce's life story would not only introduce me to new spiritual concepts, but it would also present me with a model for being helpful to others—an amazing spiritual gift of assisting others to find God's way in their lives. That this same kind of potential for service lay within me was the farthest thing from my mind at the time. It would be several years before I would discover what God had planned for me.

Our days at Big Bear Lake continued to be very busy, full of hard work and good fellowship with church friends. In reflecting over the many years Doris and I had spent there, we saw how our spiritual understanding had unfolded. We had started from a fundamentalist view, moving into the baptism in the Holy Spirit, the gifts of the Spirit, and becoming active in charismatic groups. Next had come a greater understanding of God's infinite grace, and now a belief in the soul's growth through reincarnation. Being an engineer, I progressed in a very orderly way, one step at a time.

After seven years at Big Bear Lake, one morning during our quiet time, a verse in our Bible reading stood out with a startling message: " . . . Arise, and go thou and thine household, and sojourn wheresoever thou canst sojourn: for the Lord hath called for a famine; and it shall also come upon the land seven years." (II Kings 8:1) To us the message was clear. It was time to move on.

During our stay at Big Bear Lake, Doris and I had always felt that our position at the lodge was that of caretaker. God was the true owner. So when we considered leaving, we felt we should place it in the hands of a church who appreciated its value as a retreat center. One church in particular, which had utilized our facilities for its youth groups, was located in North Hollywood. We prayed about the situation at great length and felt comfortable donating the lodge to them, completely furnished. They accepted and with great joy the transfer was made.

In November 1968 we moved our personal belongings down off the mountain and into a new rented house in Redlands, only a few minutes from my office at Norton Air Force Base. The following week the mountains experienced one of their worst snowstorms, with news reports of twenty-foot snowdrifts. I was glad that we were no longer at Big Bear Lake!

We had left that life behind and waited anxiously to see what new and exciting adventures God had in store for us. We didn't have to wait long.

Chapter Twelve
Healing of Memories

S hortly after moving to Redlands, even greater gifts from God were revealed to me and more wonderful doors opened. It all started after Doris enrolled in a seven-week course called "Adventures in Reality." After each class she shared her adventures with me. Some of them were familiar, such as the baptism in the Holy Spirit, but one adventure especially stood out: guided meditation. This was a new experience for Doris, and she came home full of wonder. She explained to me what she had learned, and she led me in the same guided meditation she had just gone through. This turned out to be as meaningful to me as it had been to her. We soon had an opportunity to apply the method to a puzzling situation.

The house we had rented was in a new construction area in a cul-de-sac at the edge of an orange grove. It had a large dining room. Since we had included our dining room furniture in the donation of the lodge at Big Bear Lake, we began looking for a set to replace it.

In an antique store Doris found a dining room furniture set that she really liked. It consisted of a china cabinet, a credenza, a large table, and six big beautiful, heavy chairs. I said we ought to buy it—it was everything that we needed. While Doris agreed, she was very hesitant, almost afraid. When I suggested the purchase, she confessed to a feeling of uneasiness. She just didn't feel right about it. There was no doubt that she liked it, but that uncomfortable feeling persisted. This went on for a couple of months, and finally we decided to do something about it. We had begun to wonder if there could be something from one of her past lives that had surfaced, creating this hesitancy. We agreed to explore that possibility.

One morning in January 1969, I led Doris on a guided meditation and asked her to project herself back in time to where the same feeling of uneasiness might occur. I instructed her to let me know when she started to have those feelings and to describe where she found herself. I meditated with her and I, independently in meditation, journeyed back in time, arriving at a place in Rome, Italy, where an auction was taking place.

No sooner was I aware of that place than Doris told me that she had reached a time where the same uneasiness gripped her. Amazingly she, too, was aware of an auction taking place. I asked her to describe everything she saw. "They are selling furniture—it's mine," she said as she started to sob. "They are selling all my possessions. That's all I have." She continued crying.

Then she told me that she was seeing herself as a slave, carried by the Roman army from another country back to Rome. She had been allowed to take with her just a few personal possessions, and now they were being sold. The money from the sale went to the auctioneer and to an army officer who was standing close by.

She described the entire scene for me, and I watched the auction as she was telling me about it. I asked her

to look at the army officer. As she followed my suggestion, she saw him turn to look at her. I directed Doris
to step up to the auctioneer and then to the army officer, one at a time, and forgive them. This she did.

Next I informed Doris in the guided meditation that
it was necessary for her to go see the emperor also and
forgive him. This was very difficult for her, and she
didn't want to do it. The mere thought caused all the
strength in her legs to give out, and she became very
weak. I suggested she look to her right where Jesus
was standing. Seeing Him, she asked Him to help her.
With her right hand she reached up and grasped His
shoulder for support. Leaning on Him in this way, they
walked together to see the emperor. Doris continued to
weep from fear at the thought of having to face him.
Jesus placed His arm around her to further support
her as they moved. All the while in my own meditation,
I was able to observe what was going on.

Entering the emperor's chamber, all Doris could see
was a huge throne and a large man sitting on it. She
was so afraid of him that she could raise her eyes only
to the level of his knees. But I urged her to look him in
the eyes and tell him that she forgave him for making
her a prisoner. After several attempts she was able to
look into the emperor's eyes, and she forgave him.

Then she told me that although there was no audi-
ble conversation between them, the look in the
emperor's eyes was one of helplessness. They seemed
to say, "This is one of the tragedies of war, and I'm
sorry that it had to happen." Leaving the emperor,
Doris walked in a normal manner with Jesus at her
side; the strength in her legs had returned.

This seemed to conclude the healing of that painful
memory, so I brought her back to the present time,
1969.

Doris' emotional conflict from the Roman era had surfaced from her subconscious mind and had deeply influenced her modern-day feelings and actions. From the healing meditation she received a new understanding of wartime situations. What's more, that uneasy feeling about purchasing the dining room furniture was gone. She now felt free of the burden of that past-life trauma. As a result, a few days later we bought the furniture.

From this experience we began to realize that healing memories of the distant past could be a very powerful tool for getting to the source of unresolved conflicts. It quickly brought to mind an inner conflict I hadn't been able to resolve. It had to do with the biblical teaching that we should love one another. I could love almost anyone, but it was a real problem when it came to the Japanese people.

For many years—in fact, for as long as I could remember—I had had a prejudice toward the Japanese that I could neither reconcile nor explain. Now that we were learning to heal past memories, I decided to find out why I had developed such a dislike for the Japanese. Vividly I remembered how much I despised them when I was in Japan during the Korean War. I didn't like their language, their music, and, least of all, their customs. I was furious at them for being so strange and unfriendly. On the other hand I wasn't friendly to them, either. I made no attempt to befriend them because I rejected the idea of having these seemingly strange people as my friends.

I couldn't remember that any one of them had ever done anything to me personally, so I supposed that my hostility and animosity were a result of their attack on Pearl Harbor. But after Doris' past-life meditation experience, I began to wonder if my problem could have roots in a lifetime long ago.

One day in May 1969 I projected myself back during a meditation session. I traveled to what must have been my immediate past life and found myself in England in the 1860s. I was a prosperous merchant and had made arrangements with a sailing vessel for my passage to Australia for a business trip. En route the ship ran into a violent storm in the Pacific Ocean, driving the vessel far to the north. The wind and waves battered the ship relentlessly, and eventually it capsized. Japanese fishermen found me clinging to debris and calling for help. They picked me up and brought me to shore, where I was arrested and thrown into a crowded prison. Several months went by in that rat-infested, dark, and unsanitary hole. I survived on a small bowl of unsavory food and water that was passed to me once a day. Eventually, I was released and sailed back to England, never getting to Australia. (Later, I remembered that while living in San Diego I had a great desire to visit Australia. This past life helped explain that, too.)

The recall of this past-life experience brought to light the source of my aversion toward the Japanese. I had been mistreated, and my subconscious mind wouldn't let me forget it. If I could forgive my Japanese captors, I would be free from that limiting soul memory—what is called in the Orient "karma." The words of Jesus kept running through my mind: "And ye shall know the truth, and the truth shall make you free." (John 8:32)

The truth of the matter had been finally revealed to me. I immediately forgave those who had held me in prison. Instantly, I felt great relief and peace over this traumatic situation. It was as if a light had been turned on within me. I no longer felt angry toward the Japanese; rather, I felt a strong urge to know these people better. I longed to cultivate an interest in their music, language, and culture. (Although it would be still many years in the future, that opportunity came in 1977, when Doris and I traveled to Japan. At that time I felt no strangeness among them and no hostility toward them. There was instead joy, great interest, and pleasure in just being there.)

In that same meditation in May 1969—almost as a bonus—I discovered the source of my longstanding fascination with Mendelssohn's Overture to A *Midsummer Night's Dream*. I saw that I had been an amateur musician in my spare time, playing the violin in a small orchestra in England. Those years had been a very pleasant period in that particular lifetime. While playing in that orchestra, I first heard this piece of music by Mendelssohn. During my Japanese imprisonment, strains of that overture played over and over in my mind, helping me to maintain my sanity and to survive that difficult experience.

It had been as a teenager in pre-war Norway in the late 1930s that this fascination surfaced in my current lifetime. I went to a movie theater to see A *Midsummer Night's Dream*. I was sixteen years old and had no idea what the movie was about. From the beginning to the end of the film, I sat spellbound. The music sounded so familiar; yet, I didn't recall ever having heard it.

On the way home, I whistled every passage of the entire score, and I pictured in my mind each instrument as it played a particular passage of the score. Although I didn't understand how or why, yet on an inner level I knew that somehow I must have been very familiar with that composition at some time, but then I didn't trouble myself about where or when it might have been, for the concept of reincarnation hadn't entered my head. I always remembered that movie; and it was brought back vividly to my memory every time I heard the overture. But I had never been able to answer the question of where I had heard it before. This Japanese incident seemed to present the answer.

This experience gave me clear evidence that a problem from a past life can block growth in the present lifetime. From personal knowledge I understand the wisdom of the old saying that when we hold resentment and other negative emotions in our minds and hearts, we keep alive that which will eventually destroy us.

As I found out, simply confronting the troublesome symptom can be a dead-end. However, when the *source* of a problem is revealed, it's easier to resolve that conflict. In this case, the resolution came when I forgave those who were involved. Then I could move on. What's more, this healing experience opened up my understanding to the importance of resolving inner conflicts. Like all of us, unresolved problems tend to move in and out of consciousness as a thread being woven into a fabric, developing a pattern of disharmony in my life. With my prejudice against the Japanese the source of a conflict came from the distant past, but it could nevertheless be dealt with and transformed right here in this lifetime. All this impressed upon Doris and me the importance of finding the source of any negative emotion and dealing with it by asking for and extending forgiveness.

Since moving away from Big Bear Lake, we hadn't joined any other place of worship. We discovered that fundamental Christians would have very little to do with us after they knew what we had come to believe. Once in a while, though, we would attend a church service.

A couple from one of our former prayer groups refused even to come to our home for a visit. When we invited them, they told us that we were in error and, therefore, they couldn't have fellowship with us. That hurt, for we had been close, but we tried to understand their position as well.

We were out in a desert of isolation with no place to go on Sunday mornings. I had wanted to teach Sunday school but that was denied me. Though I tried to tell the ministers and lay people alike that I still believed in Christ—I hadn't dropped my faith in Him but had only gone a little further in my belief—it was like talking to a wall. If believing in the baptism in the Holy Spirit didn't give us a "bad name," accepting the concept of reincarnation was sure to do it.

Nevertheless, we were able to find a small prayer group with whom we could have some fellowship and prayer time. It certainly wasn't the same, however, as attending a worship service and being members of a church. Doris and I have always felt this loss deeply and have been saddened by our forced separation from these influences, but we have never doubted that the path we chose was part of God's plan.

In addition to the prayer group, I was still active in the Full Gospel Businessmen's Fellowship. Then Doris and I became active in another group which proved to be as influential in my life and growth as the other groups. This was a charismatic group composed mostly of those of us who had gone through the "Adventures in Reality" series. Both of these groups steered us into a closer walk with God and a more effective outreach.

The charismatic group held weekend retreats in the San Francisco Bay area. Doris and I flew there for the meetings. We attended classes on dream interpretation, baptism in the Holy Spirit, and the gifts of the

Spirit, prayer, meditation, and whatever else the con-
ferees needed for further growth.

As we became more proficient in these subjects ourselves, we longed for this opportunity to be made
available to our friends in southern California. I offered to make the arrangements for retreats in our area
if the leaders would come and present their program.
They agreed.

I phoned key people in the greater Los Angeles area
to notify them of the meetings to be arranged. Two
hundred people attended. It was a wonderful spiritual
experience, and they demanded more. We were happy
to oblige. Doris and I led some of the classes as well.
What had begun as an exciting learning experience for
us became a rewarding opportunity to serve.

For the most part, this period of time while we were
living in Redlands was totally filled by my engineering
job, being a companion to Doris, and my quest for spiritual enlightenment. But in early 1969, I decided to
take up a hobby. I was going to be an artist—the next
Rembrandt maybe!

I had always wondered how an artist got the paint
from the tube to the canvas, and now I was going to
find out. Evening classes in oil painting were being offered at a local high school, so Doris and I enrolled. We
bought the best paint and brushes, enrolled in an artist book club, and expected great results. I spent about
an hour each evening practicing the exercises. With
much help from Doris and the instructor, I thought I
did pretty well and was proud of my paintings. Years
later I looked back and recognized that this high regard and appreciation for my work wasn't shared by
others. The nicest compliment I ever received on any of
my paintings was that the frame was very nice!

While I enjoyed these classes immensely, sadly I

didn't become another Rembrandt. Nevertheless, this hobby released a dormant creative energy within me which previously hadn't been allowed to flow. Somehow, those classes helped free me. This new flow of creative energy liberated my spirit—contributing to the spiritual and psychic experiences that were soon to follow. Painting enhanced my ability to utilize the spiritual gifts that were being slowly revealed to me. This new release of creative energy didn't directly cause the psychic awakening, rather it was a valuable stepping-stone along the spiritual path. It led me to the threshold of the next door. That new opening was to a path of greater service to others. In order to help others, I was being given many tools.

Continued spiritual growth remained the top priority in my life. I was about to embark upon a new journey which involved leaping from the edge of all the light I had known into an unknown cosmos. It was a matter of trusting to be taught how to fly.

CHAPTER THIRTEEN
LEARNING TO FLY

L ittle did I realize when I came home from the office that day in the late spring of 1969 that my life was about to change dramatically. A phenomenon would occur during the next few minutes that would alter my destiny. That particular evening I had come home from a hectic day at my engineering office in San Bernardino. I was tired, irritable, and hungry. The only thing on my mind was dinner, followed by rest and relaxation. But Doris had other plans.

Earlier in the day, a letter had arrived at our home from a young man who needed guidance. He faced a choice among several job offers. He didn't know which one to take, so he asked if I could get a message from God concerning his dilemma. Though we had never met, I supposed that either he had heard me lecture somewhere, or he may have learned from others that I sometimes got messages from God.

In any case, Doris believed his letter had a sense of urgency, and it deserved an answer at once. But being tired and hungry, I wasn't easily convinced. I simply stated in as calm a voice as I could that I'd rather wait until *after* dinner because I'd feel better then. Nevertheless, she suggested that I could at least pray for an answer while she finished preparing the meal. What she was really telling me was that there wouldn't be any dinner until I had found an answer for this young man.

So I sat down in my favorite rocking chair, took a deep breath, and relaxed. I quieted myself and started to pray for him. I'd prayed for people in need many times before. But this time something dramatically different happened.

Immediately I was out of my body, atop the roof of my home. Looking around, I saw the tall eucalyptus trees a few hundred feet away, the orange grove directly behind me, and to my right and left the other homes in the cul-de-sac where we lived. With some sort of penetrating vision, I looked down through the rafters and saw my body sitting in the rocking chair in my living room. I thought to myself how interesting it was to be in two places at once.

However, I sensed there must be a reason for being out of my body, so I pushed off from the roof and soared upward, continuing to pray for the young man. Soon I found myself walking along a narrow path, barely wide enough for one person. The path and the surrounding area were like soft, white, billowing clouds.

It was extremely still, like after a snowfall when nature is covered with a gentle hush. Walking in solitude, I was filled with reverence for God. The sacred silence permeated my being.

As I walked along I knew somehow that I was on my way to get information which might help this young man. Although it was a unique and unfamiliar experience, I felt neither fear nor apprehension. Everything felt comfortable, as if I knew exactly what I was doing. Coming to a fork in the path, I intuitively bore to the left, then veered slightly to the right around the bend.

Suddenly, I saw it.

Stopping, I gazed into the distance upon a Grecian temple-like palace with eight large columns supporting the roof. The entire structure was fashioned from pure white marble. Though I had never seen it before, somehow it looked familiar. I understood at once that this was the place where the chronicles of each person's many lives are recorded—the Akashic records.

The temple towered high above me, disappearing into the cloud banks. As I was still afar off, I longed to be there. Instantly, I found myself standing just in front of the vast, marble platform where the Grecian columns reached skyward. The platform was about two feet above the level where I was standing. I knew that the information I was seeking was inside this building, so I stepped up onto the platform.

As I climbed up, two men dressed in white togas appeared and welcomed me. One declared that they had been waiting for me and that they were my guides. I told them about the young man's dilemma. They suggested that perhaps something from his past lives could give a clue to help him work out his problem. That possibility had never occurred to me, but it made sense.

Without hesitation they ushered me into the temple's enormous library where huge bookshelves, ranging twenty to thirty feet high and separated by eight- to ten-foot aisles, extended as far as I could see. While the floors were like clouds, nevertheless they supported everything and provided firm footing.

Enormous leather-bound books of various colors, trimmed and edged with gold, filled the shelves. To me the sight was awe-inspiring. I had spent considerable time in numerous libraries, but I had never seen anything like this.

As we walked down the aisles, my guides selected specific books and carried them to a very large table. There, they opened them and supplied the answers I sought. Intrigued by the beautiful calligraphy on the pages, I had to force myself to concentrate on the information being given to me. When my guides finished, they closed the books and returned them to the shelves, and we left the library with the data I needed to pass on to the young man.

My guides escorted me to the place where I had entered, and I said goodbye with an inner knowing that I would return. Retracing my steps along the cloud-like path, I stepped off into space. Like jumping off a diving board into a swimming pool, I drifted downward. Although it felt as if I were falling rapidly, it was serene — there was no sensation of rushing wind against my body.

In the twinkling of an eye I was again standing on my roof and could see myself in the rocking chair below. Quickly, I slipped into my physical body. I was home.

As soon as I opened my eyes, Doris announced that dinner was ready.

It seemed to me that I had been gone at least an hour, but a glance at my watch revealed that only five minutes had elapsed!

During the meal I calmly recounted my experience to Doris. As unusual as this experience was for us, Doris and I weren't especially surprised by this event. We both considered this another step in our spiritual growth. Later, Doris admitted to having felt a tingling emotion in her solar plexus area when I told her where I had been — momentary delight over this evidence of new growth in me. We were both thankful that God was still working in us.

We sent the information I received from the Akashic records to the young man. Later, he responded, writing that he had found the suggestions very helpful and timely.

What a change this experience initiated in my life!

Someone once said that change is at times desirable, even necessary occasionally, but always to be expected. In my case, it was time for a change—in my outlook, my consciousness, my understanding, and in the further application of the principles I had known. In all this I found it essential to keep Christ central in my life.

When Doris and I first started on our conscious search for God in 1953, neither of us had heard of out-of-body experiences or the Akashic records. We weren't even vaguely familiar with the concepts of reincarnation and karma. It was foreign to what we believed in our fundamental Christian philosophy. There was simply no room for the notion of past lives and astral projection.

In time, we had found ourselves living in an intellectual religious utopia, and because of years of studying the scriptures we thought we knew the counsel and plan of God. It was the most remote item from my mind that someday I would be going to the Akashic records and giving psychic readings.

Yet today, I believe that this initial visit to those records uprooted me out of my paradise, and God used it as a new plow to break up the fallow ground of my understanding of His ways and His love.

Now, the question in my mind was this: Had I become flexible enough in my orthodox Christianity to allow for the transition that lay ahead? I shared my Akashic experience with a small prayer group made up of a few of those who had attended the "Adventures" series with Doris. I phoned our minister friend who lived in the San Francisco Bay area. He agreed with me that this was just another form of service that God had made available to me. As a matter of fact, he was one of the first handful of friends to request that I go to the Akashic records on his behalf.

He called one day, saying that he had been counseling a young housewife for several months but was now unable to make any further progress. She had two children and, as she described it, a wonderful husband. They lived in a well-to-do neighborhood, and seemingly everything was fine. Except, she had a secret problem.

She had attempted suicide several times because she just didn't like her husband, and she couldn't understand why. Suicide was her way of escaping from the situation. The pastor asked if I could do a reading for her to see if any information could be made available to help her. When he had finished stating his request, I immediately protested because I had never before been asked to help someone in such a condition. I didn't know if I could do it. I tried to decline, but he insisted. He was obviously concerned that there might be another suicide attempt soon. Reluctantly, I agreed at least to try.

Sitting in my comfortable chair, I began praying for this woman just as I had for the young man. I felt myself slip out of my body. Following a pathway that was now becoming very familiar to me, I arrived at the Akashic records. Here my guides helped again. The information I received showed that at one time she had lived in India, a member of a very influential and wealthy family. At a very early age she married a man much older than she. The marriage had been prearranged—a common occurrence—by the parents from the time she was born.

To her the marriage was an absolute disaster. She grew to hate her husband, found no purpose in living, and tried to kill herself several times. But each time she was unsuccessful. Her husband during that lifetime in India was the same one she was married to in this present life.

I dictated all that I had seen and learned onto a cassette tape and sent it to my friend, who hoped to use it to help this woman. As soon as the tape arrived, he made arrangements for another counseling session with her. She listened to the tape and immediately identified with the young bride in India. As she listened, she started to cry and realized that the memory from the past had been carried over to the present time. She had the same feelings and needs then as now. The hopelessness and emptiness were still with her.

She now knew the source of her despair. With help from the pastor she could forgive her parents in that past life, her husband, and herself. The minister counseled her about the attitude she held toward her marriage in India and how that might prevent her from having a successful marriage in the present. According to our pastor friend, her memory from the past was eventually healed. After that, she no longer had difficulty with that part of her life. Her relationship with her husband improved, and she was like a new person.

Needless to say, I was gratified to have been able to help someone whom I had never seen nor known. As people came to me with their needs and longings, I stretched myself a little further to help them. To serve God more fervently and humanity more effectively has always been my desire.

Within a year, these initial experiences developed

into what Doris and I have called life readings. These events took place while I was still employed in the aerospace field, so I didn't have much time to develop this new spiritual capability. But I saw it as an instrument of God to be used to help people understand themselves and their lives on this earth plane—a way of helping them become better acquainted with God. Since 1969, every time someone contacts me for help, I retrace my steps to the Akashic records—and, as of this writing, that's been over 7,000 times.

It wasn't an overnight development—it came a little at a time. Each experience with God taught me something wonderful in the way of trust and confidence, caution and discernment. I learned that the spiritual disciplines of Bible reading and prayer were important in my life. I found that my attitudes and behaviors must follow the spiritual principles I had discovered through these disciplines. I made a daily conscious effort to *be* what I believed. I haven't always succeeded, but I will continue this effort for the rest of my life.

In the meantime, while all these exciting changes were taking place, the mundane details of life continued. Our year's lease on the rental house in Redlands neared an end. We had been praying for sometime to find the right place to buy. Finally, we purchased a home in the hills of Colton. This was even closer to my office, less than five minutes' drive to work.

After we were settled, a visiting friend saw our prayer map. Her attention was drawn to the picture of a house which we had placed there seven or eight months earlier. It was high on a hill with lots of windows. She remarked that this new home and the picture on our prayer map were almost identical. Doris and I agreed. We explained that when we can find a picture similar to what we're praying for, we place it on the prayer map. Then when we look at it every day, we pray, "Thank You, Father, for this or something even better." Not only had we found the type of house we wanted within less than a year, but it had also become available just as the lease on the home in Redlands expired.

Living in Colton brought events into my surroundings which changed my perspective and caused life to be more demanding. One of these demands involved a serious health problem for Doris—and I was at a loss for how to help her.

CHAPTER FOURTEEN
TRYING OUR NEW WINGS

For over two years Doris had suffered from a nerve reaction which caused her entire body to feel as if her skin were "crawling." There was no relief for her, and the sensation was worse when she was quiet, especially at nighttime. This condition kept her awake almost all night, every night. She felt fortunate if she could sleep even a couple of hours, and she was constantly exhausted.

Because she avoided seeing a doctor except for serious illnesses, she was reluctant to consult one about this condition. Her suffering continued, even though I had prayed many times for some relief for her. I became quite discouraged and was troubled that I wasn't able to help her.

Whenever she went shopping, she had to find a parking space as close as possible to the entrance door so that she wouldn't have to walk too far. She was totally worn down, and any extra exertion on her part would cause her to cry. Life for her became very difficult. She tried to hide her discomfort, but I knew she was suffering.

After I began doing readings for other people, she asked if I would do one for her. I thought about it, and

my initial reaction was not to do it. I had never done a
health reading. Besides, I wasn't sure if it was right for
me to use this new ability to benefit Doris and myself.
Her request for help changed to pleading. She reminded me that I had obtained useful information for
others, so couldn't I please try a reading for her? I told
her again I wasn't sure if I could obtain anything worthwhile. But she insisted that at least I should try. I still
resisted because I was afraid.

Finally, Doris demanded, "Aron, I'm climbing the
walls. You've *got* to try to get some help for me." What
else could I do? I put aside my fears.

With no one else present for this event, only Doris
taking notes, I went to the Akashic records and discussed the problem with my guides. The information
received was very simple. It told her to eliminate caffeine, ice cream, and other sugary substances. She was
to use fresh or canned V-8 or tomato juice for three
days. The information further stated that within three
days she would be able to sleep normally and all the
discomfort with her skin would disappear.

The reading was done in the morning. That very day
Doris started a diet exclusively of tomato or V-8 juice.
Amazingly, we saw immediate results. That night, for
the first time in over two years, she slept all the way
through until morning. After two more days of the juice
diet, her symptoms were gone and never returned. For
some time thereafter Doris was very careful about her
diet and always included V-8 juice daily. She mini-
mized her intake of caffeine and sweets for many years.
The wonderful results she obtained helped me to over-
come my fears of doing health readings.

As we shared with our prayer and Bible study
groups what God was doing in our lives, the word
spread rapidly that I was able to do readings, and more

and more people requested them. In those days we didn't have a questionnaire for them to report back to us on their reading. Being very busy with my office work and prayer group activities, we didn't have time to follow-up in any way. But the fact that people were recommending me to others had to mean that they were satisfied with the information they had received. I felt that this was establishing a track record for me as each new request came in.

One lady in particular taught us a very interesting and meaningful lesson which we have never forgotten. After she had received the cassette tape of her reading, she dropped by to visit and wanted to give us some money. But I protested, saying that I didn't need the money. I had a good position in the aerospace industry, and the reading was free. She wouldn't hear of it.

With that she handed Doris $20. She reasoned that I had utilized a special kind of energy for that reading, something she couldn't do. But she could return the energy in a different form—the $20. She explained that all this was simply an exchange of energy, and sharing this way would help the energy flow.

To me this was a unique and beautiful way of expressing her understanding about energy, and I agreed to accept her generous gift. She was a woman of deep convictions, and I appreciated her feeling responsible to do what she felt was right.

Her thoughts about responsibilities reminded me that I still had the obligation to finish recording the New Testament in Hebrew. Almost two years ago, while living at Big Bear Lake, I had started the project. I began to feel an urgency to complete that work as soon as possible. It was as if my internal clock were telling me that time was short. By working every evening I was able to complete it in forty-five days. I experienced a great sense of accomplishment and hoped the tape recordings would be helpful to those who would receive them in Israel.

Weeks later, Doris told me that she missed the special atmosphere that came over the house while the Hebrew words were being recorded. It was like a holy hush settling in the air. "My inner being felt deeply uplifted after each session," she confided. I had the same experience and supposed that the "vibrations" from the words were what I was feeling. It was a clear lesson to me on the powerful influence of vibrations.

Another strong influence on me was my dream life. Doris and I were particularly interested in working with them for guidance. It was a fascinating growth experience. Understanding dreams was like learning a new language—except this language was in symbols. We each started to keep a dream journal and became better acquainted with that part of our beings. We were always ready for a new challenge, and after we studied and worked with the subject for a while, we conducted classes on dream interpretation at several weekend retreats.

I had long been impressed with a verse from the Old Testament: "For God speaketh once, yea twice, yet man perceiveth it not. In a dream, in a vision of the night, when deep sleep falleth upon men, in slumberings upon the bed; then he openeth the ears of men, and sealeth their instruction, that he may withdraw man from his purpose, and hide pride from man." (Job 33:14-17)

It was evident from the Bible and writers like Carl Jung that dreams contained material of substance to which we should pay attention.

One night I had a dream which gave me notice that

a change was coming. It took place on March 17, 1970. My journal reads:

"Saw an old man with a gray suit and wide-brimmed burly hat sitting on a rock beside a road. His face was weather-beaten, but it was kind and gentle. He was talking explicitly to me though there were many other people around me and many others walking on the road. The day was either at its end or just before sun-up, because it wasn't quite light.

"I could see the man's face. I was a boy ten to twelve years old. The man was saying to me, 'There is coming a change in your life,' and he smiled and showed great love. I knew he meant a change in my occupation. He spoke with authority and power, and I knew he was in charge. I also asked him if there was a move, physical, to the north. But he didn't answer; or perhaps answered, and I didn't hear it because of the noise around me."

I interpreted this dream to refer to my retirement from my work—which would be in sixteen years. Something Doris and I had been thinking about as an option was to buy into a franchise business if I took an early retirement. But there was nothing, as far as I could see, in the way of an immediate change.

I didn't think much about the dream after that—office duties and working on my spiritual growth occupied me. In fact, my job at TRW kept me as busy as I had ever been. However, in early April 1970 I began hearing rumors that a number of government contracts had been canceled. There was a possibility that some engineers might be laid off. I felt secure in my position and paid the rumors little attention. God had protected me before in my career, and I was sure He would do the same now.

On Friday, April 24, I had lunch with an engineer I had known for many years. We had become close friends. He was also a member of the home-based Bible class at Redlands which I had been asked to teach. He informed me that he had seen a directive from top management. There would be a reduction in the engineering staff. Hearing this, I reminded myself of the verse from the book of Psalms: "A thousand shall fall at thy side, and ten thousand at thy right hand; but it shall not come nigh thee." (Psalm 91:7) I was confident that this forthcoming layoff would not touch me. How wrong I was!

That afternoon I was called into the supervisor's office and told that because of the loss of contracts I would be laid off. My last day would be Friday, May 22. I was also not required to work between that day and May 22. He told me that for the next thirty days all the facilities of the company—including secretarial services, long-distance phone calls, and copying services—would be at my disposal. This was to help me locate a new position. Although this was a very generous offer, I was at a loss for words. I thanked him for that provision and left.

Back in my office I sat, mulling over this shocking news. I told myself not to be overly concerned. After all, I had contacts in the industry all over the country. Surely it wouldn't be too long before I would find an even better position. I hoped that it would be before my time at TRW ran out.

Suddenly, the old man in my dream came to mind. This must be what he meant concerning the change coming into my life. Only one month had gone by since that dream, and already I faced that change. (On looking back, it's obvious that originally I hadn't been willing to accept the real message of the dream.) I locked up my secret documents, cleared off my desk, and left for home.

Doris picked me up that night from the office. She was waiting for me as I came out. I had hardly closed the car door when I told her that I was being laid off. I didn't want her to be concerned since I was sure I'd find another position very soon. Reassuring me, she replied that she wasn't worried. Something better would come along.

Then she told me that a package had arrived for me that day. It was from a lady we had met at a spiritual retreat in the San Francisco Bay area, but Doris hadn't opened it. I thought that receiving such a package was curious because we hadn't seen or heard from that woman in about two years. In fact, our only contact with her had been at those meetings.

As soon as I got home, I started to open the square, thin package. It couldn't be a book, I thought, as I un-wrapped it. What else would people send me? It was a recording entitled "It's a Brand-New Day" by a group of Jesuit seminarians. The arrival of this thoughtful gift was quite synchronistic and appropiate.

Yes, this certainly was a brand-new day for me. Since Doris and I hadn't corresponded with her, we concluded that God must have told her that I would need some encouragement. I got her phone number from the operator and called to thank her for such a timely gift. She said that she had bought the record for herself, played it, and was persuaded that I would like to hear it, too. She had purchased another one and sent it to me. She had listened to God's inner prompt-ing and responded at the right time. It reassured and encouraged me to know that God was moving on my behalf already.

Soon thereafter another timely encouragement came from supportive friends. A couple from the Bible class I taught called to say they had heard about my layoff at TRW. They had a cassette tape they thought we should hear and wanted to bring it over after dinner. Again, God was working. Doris and I were so grateful. The message on the tape was right to the point: When God closes one door, He opens another.

Over that weekend Doris and I spent most of the time in prayer and Bible reading, seeking guidance as to what the approach should be for next week. I knew that it would be different from any previous week. I had to find another job as soon as possible.

Monday morning at the office I started revising my resume. I called companies all over the country and talked to a number of people in top management. I knew them personally and explained my situation. Each time the reply was the same. They were in an identical situation. Contract cancellations had hit the defense industry on all levels. Unfortunately, there wasn't anything they could do to help me.

I followed up on leads from my co-workers, but everything came to a dead-end. The newspapers reported that there were 60,000 engineers out of work in the Los Angeles area alone. Even those with doctorate degrees were driving taxicabs or pumping gasoline. I knew then that it was going to be tough to find employment. Fortunately, I still had a whole month before my days with TRW were over.

I contacted a professional recruiting firm in Los Angeles. Three times a week I drove the ninety miles into Los Angeles and conferred with the recruiting agency. They were encouraging and reassured me that the search had only started. But all too soon the thirty days came to an end. On Friday May 22, 1970, I left the company. Gone was all the security which I had enjoyed for so many years. Now I was on my own.

Over the next three months Doris and I wrote and

mailed out over 300 letters in response to job openings. Out of all those letters, I received only one interview and that didn't materialize into a job. I wasn't surprised. There were 5,000 applicants for every opening.

Throughout this period I took a hard look at the recent years of my life. I remembered giving up my job in San Diego in 1962 to move to Big Bear Lake. I was without regular employment, and three months later I had to go back because of financial reasons. That had led me to believe that God wanted me to stay in engineering for the rest of my life. Like Paul the Apostle, I decided then that I'd do religious work in my spare time. (Paul made tents for a living in every city along his missionary journeys. In his spare time he ministered to the people in whatever city he found himself.) I had adjusted my thinking to reflect that new sense of my destiny; however, I was willing to do whatever God wanted.

Now I was out of a job and the prospects for new employment weren't hopeful. I couldn't understand it. What else was there for me to do? The only work I knew was engineering. I had believed for many years that I would make my living as an engineer and die an engineer.

It was a very difficult time for me. I was hurting. Emotionally, I was very insecure; intellectually, I felt betrayed and rejected. I did feel very strong spiritually but that hadn't produced new employment for me.

Leaving my job in San Diego hadn't been so difficult. At that time I was in control of what I was doing. I had made the decision to leave. To be laid off was so much more difficult because somebody else was in charge. I was pushed out when I wanted to stay. I was on the outside wanting desperately to get in. But the door was locked, and it appeared to me that it was nailed shut.

By now my dreams reflected the trauma I was enduring. Often I dreamed that I was working at TRW and was told I was going to be laid off. Upon hearing this, I would cry and wake up crying. My subconscious mind wouldn't let go of my job. Consciously, I felt the same way—I just wouldn't release that job.

Doris was a very dear and close companion to me during this trial. Her comfort and encouragement was unceasing. Without her I don't think I would have been able to hold up during those difficult and painful times. Thursdays were especially painful. That was the day I had previously received my paycheck. It was one of the many things I missed. When I talked to Doris about it, she would reassure me, saying that soon I would have a paycheck again. It sounded good, but where would it come from?

As time passed, the job market became a dim hope. Finally, by the end of July, I had to admit that finding an engineering job with a new company wasn't going to happen. I was nearing the end of my rope.

For weeks Doris had tried to get my attention. She kept repeating that there was something else I could do. I didn't want to hear what she had to say because I was determined to climb back on the ship called engineering. But with my admission of failure, I finally listened to her.

Quite simply, she suggested that I could do readings full-time. That could be my next career. I thought about it for five seconds and said "No!" She didn't give up. She reminded me how many people I had already been able to help by doing readings while I was still working in the aerospace field. By giving myself full-time to this work, how many more people would I be able to help?

I thought about it. Reluctantly, I suggested that I might do the readings in the interim until another engineering position was offered. That was agreeable to Doris.

Doris and I told a few people we knew that I would be giving readings full-time now. These individuals were leaders of prayer groups. We explained that there would be no specified charge for the readings and that whatever people wanted to donate would be accepted.

Within a short time several requests for readings came in the mail. People were very gracious because they had enclosed a donation with each request. But I was still searching for a job. Giving readings was only temporary, I believed. I was feeling very insecure from not having a steady paycheck or health insurance.

On August 17, Doris took the initiative. She wrote a letter to Hugh Lynn Cayce of the Association for Research and Enlightenment in Virginia Beach, Virginia. She told him that reading about the life of his father, Edgar Cayce, had been somewhat of a turning point in our lives. Briefly, she explained that I was able to go to the Akashic records and obtain information to help people and that now she and others had persuaded me to devote full-time to giving readings.

She presented examples of what I had done and how helpful the readings had been. She offered to give him names and addresses if he would like to check. Then she closed by asking for any advice he might have for us and for ways we might make our work known to others.

On September 1 he wrote his reply: "Thank you for your letter of August 17. I am most interested in the description you gave in your letter of the readings which are being given by your husband. First, I have a number of questions and then at the first opportunity,

I would like to see and talk with you both." He asked questions about how I obtained the information from the records, what I saw when I was there, and how we kept files on what we got.

Hugh Lynn requested the names and addresses of those who had received readings and transcripts of their tapes so he could ask them pertinent questions. Then he closed with, "You know the old story about building better mousetraps. I'm sure you'll have no difficulty at all reaching a larger and larger group of people with such information if it continues to prove interesting and helpful. I'll have many suggestions as we get into further discussion on this matter."

Needless to say, Doris and I were greatly impressed by the interest Hugh Lynn Cayce was showing in our work and my readings. We eagerly anticipated the next step with him.

By mid-September Doris and I had decided to take a reading on our situation and see if we could obtain direction as to where we should live. The information we received was very helpful as well as comforting. My guides suggested that we move in three steps. First, to Santa Maria to be near family. Doris' mother and two sisters lived in that area. We were to rent a place there—not buying a house because we'd be there only one year. In the second step we were to move to southern Oregon, to the Medford area, and stay there between three and five years. The third step would bring us to our last place, which was in the state of Washington, north of Seattle.

As she always did for a reading, Doris took notes as the information was given. Near the end of the reading, she asked why we couldn't go directly to Washington state, our last area. The answer from the guides was that there was much for us to learn in each place. There were people we needed to meet who would be of help to us, and along the way we would slowly establish our work.

This advice was a bit disappointing. It would have been so much easier to make one move instead of three. We accepted the information and started to pack, knowing we'd follow the guidance and go to Santa Maria.

In the meantime, Doris and I drove to Stockton where I had been asked to speak at a prayer group. Out of curiosity, we drove on to Oregon to check out the Medford area. We drove around in some of the residential areas and business sections. Frankly, we really weren't too impressed.

Once we got back from Oregon, we started on work of a high priority: keeping up the Hugh Lynn Cayce contact. We sensed that his advice was going to be crucial to our work. We obtained permission from certain people for whom I had given readings, and Doris sent another letter to Hugh Lynn Cayce with their names and addresses, as he had requested. She answered his questions in as much detail as she could and promised that we would make arrangements to meet him if he were coming to the West Coast soon.

Before long we got a letter back. He would be in Los Angeles on December 12 and asked if we could meet him at his motel that day. He commented on many of the items Doris had put in her letter, and he offered some helpful suggestions which we started following immediately. For example, he suggested that I should follow the instructions the readings gave for me personally. That reminded me of having read how Edgar Cayce's life might have been prolonged had he followed the personal suggestions from his own readings. I made a mental note to take Hugh Lynn's advice. We could hardly wait for our face-to-face meeting with him to learn more.

Two weeks before Thanksgiving we rented a U-Haul truck. We had been fortunate to find quickly a buyer for our house in Colton. Doris had gone ahead a few days earlier and rented a home in Santa Maria. She called to give me the address. With the help of friends from the Bible class in Redlands, we loaded the truck. One of the men offered to drive. That was great relief for me, so I gratefully accepted his offer. Late that day we were on our way. The first step—following guidance for me from our readings—was under way. I knew Hugh Lynn would be pleased to hear I was following his advice.

Chapter Fifteen
Seeking the Giver

My life had suddenly turned in a different direction. I was unsure whether I was comfortable with my new role as a full-time psychic counselor. Now I had a new career, in a new place—although Santa Maria wasn't totally unfamiliar to me, for I had spent many hours dating Doris while attending college in San Luis Obispo. It was here, too, that we had been married in the Santa Maria Methodist Church.

Family and friends welcomed us back. We settled in and began to do the readings from the requests that we had received while living in Colton. But in the back of my mind was the lingering discomfort that came from thinking of myself as a professional psychic. I was hoping somehow to get back to work as an engineer as soon as possible. I constantly searched the newspapers and other sources for openings, and I applied wherever I recognized a job possibility. I didn't give up, but neither did I treat lightly this new work which I had decided to undertake in the interim—doing readings. As more people heard about my psychic readings, we soon were booked for several months.

Doris and I contacted friends in the area whom we

had met at charismatic gatherings. One of these friends offered to transcribe the three sample readings so that Doris could respond to Hugh Lynn's request. Doris wrote to him saying that we would be happy to meet with him on December 12 in Los Angeles.

When we first started to do readings in Santa Maria, we allowed people to come to our home and sit in on the reading, asking any questions they might have. This proved to be very interesting for them, but it was time-consuming for us. People were so fascinated by what they heard in the reading that some stayed for many hours afterward. This procedure took a great deal of our time. We scheduled three readings every morning, at 8, 9:30, and 11:00, and we wanted to begin each reading on time. To keep to that schedule, we finally decided to forego having people present.

Even though we readily found a solution to the time-scheduling problem, another issue emerged. I had become very concerned about whether giving readings would ever supply our financial needs. I wrestled with this new problem and sought answers. Would our economic necessities be taken care of? Would I be able to earn enough from this type of service to pay our bills? I reflected on the twenty years I had spent in the aerospace field, when I had received a paycheck every week—something that had made me feel very secure. But this work into which God and Doris had launched me was different. There would be no weekly paychecks. Nothing was sure. This was a new beginning and I was frightened.

I prayed often and I talked with Doris about my fears. I had to know if what I was doing was really what God had planned for me. I needed to hear from God. And God answered, but not in a way I had expected.

One day I heard a tune playing over and over in my

head. It just came spontaneously—I hadn't heard it recently on the radio or TV. At first I didn't pay too much attention to it, but it stayed with me for a number of days. When it persisted, I decided to quiet myself and listen. The melody was the familiar "Ole Man River." Even though I heard it very clearly in my mind, I didn't know what it meant to me at that time. I asked Doris if she knew the words to that melody, and she sang them to me.

A few days later, as I kept going over the words to the song, the message became clear: "Don't worry over your concerns. Instead, like Ole Man River, just keep rolling along." Then I was reminded of a passage from the Bible: " . . . seek ye first the kingdom of God, and his righteousness; and all these things shall be added unto you." (Matthew 6:33) I knew we had been following that principle. I just needed to trust God to fulfill it.

I felt truly inspired once again. The guidance was clear: Continue with what you are doing and all your needs will be taken care of. I started letting go of my worries and concerns—although the change didn't happen overnight. I also started really trusting that God would take care of us through my new career.

A few weeks after we had moved to Santa Maria, several people approached me, asking if I would teach them how to go to the Akashic records. Doris and I invited them to meet with us and discuss it.

At that meeting I explained that I could teach them only from my own experience. I told them that my spiritual journey had begun with a commitment to God as the foundation of my life. I continued, saying that it was my conviction that the ability to give readings came as a result of that commitment. Along that journey many personal disciplines were set in motion—such as prayer, meditation, daily periods of reading and studying the Bible, memorizing scripture verses, and making myself available for service in my church and community. This helped me to understand and act on the guidance of God as I saw it in the scriptures.

All through this initial meeting I emphasized that my primary motivation for these daily personal disciplines was to become better acquainted with God, not to enable me to read the Akashic records. In perfecting those disciplines, I had been led to the Akashic records. I emphasized time and again the importance of keeping motives clear and of being honest. I suggested to them that when they eventually learned to go to the Akashic records, one priority should be uppermost: to find a useful purpose for the information to be obtained. But above everything else was the significance of dedicating themselves to God, practicing God's presence in their daily lives—whether or not it led to the temple among the clouds and the Akashic records.

I urged them to consider that in their search they should seek the Giver of all things—not only the gifts. Going to the Akashic records is not an end unto itself; it's another rung on the ladder of spiritual development. I reminded them that if they should reach the Akashic records it wouldn't mean that they had "arrived" spiritually, for I believed there is much more to life and reality beyond the Akashic records.

At the close of the meeting I reminded them again that the only way I could teach was to share what I had learned—to take them along the path I had traveled. I suggested we start with a weekly Bible study and prayer group. During the week each member would have assignments such as prayer, meditation, their own personal Bible study; and they should be alert for inner instructions about how to apply the principles they might find there.

After I finished my suggestions, they all sat there with blank stares. Nobody spoke. Interrupting the awkward pause, I stated that the first meeting would be next Tuesday evening. Anyone interested could join us then. After refreshments they left.

Tuesday evening came, and no one showed up.

Seeing that that group wasn't interested in the spiritually oriented program I had suggested for developing psychic abilities, I focused my energies on other people who, I thought, would be more receptive—individuals who were just beginning their interest in these topics. I presented a course on developing intuition. No intensive attempt was made to help those participants establish a more meaningful spiritual foundation or spiritual discipline. There was, of course, a short period of meditation at the beginning of each session and a closing prayer. But primarily this was just a fun time of discovering their intuitive abilities.

When there was an interest expressed or when an appropriate opportunity surfaced, I would present options and make several suggestions of how spiritual disciplines might be helpful. I encouraged each person to practice working with his or her intuition during the week, using the exercise I had just taught in class. At the next week's class the results of the exercise were discussed. The exercises included psychometry, the use of ESP (Zener) cards, and a partnership task that involved praying for each other during the week. There were also suggestions about meditation, private prayer, and Bible reading. To my mind I was offering in this class merely a surface-level introduction to this type of development.

During the course several people asked how long it would take to develop their intuitive abilities. They, of course, hoped it would be just a very short time. I explained that it would be different for each person. Some individuals come into this life with their intuition already strongly developed from a previous life. That could make awakening it in this life easier and faster. Regardless, I urged them not to give up, but to persist. I tried to be aware of the needs of each one in the group, and sometimes I was able to offer personalized encouragement or recommendations.

An incident with one young man from the class stands out in my mind. It was an example of someone who got immediate help from his own intuition. A few weeks before the classes ended, he moved to another town about a hundred miles south of Santa Maria. Not long after, Doris and I received a short note from him. He had been struggling with a new problem. "Last night," he wrote, "I prayed for a solution." Then he went on to say that I appeared to him in a dream and gave him a scripture verse. He immediately awoke, got his Bible and read the verse. It was the answer. So he thanked me for coming to him when he needed help. He didn't share any of the details, but I could see that he was getting the guidance he needed. Perhaps it really was me meeting him in the spiritual realm at night—or maybe I appeared in his dream as a symbol of his own inner wisdom. Either way, he was tapping a valuable resource with his intuition.

On December 12, Doris and I left Santa Maria very early to meet Hugh Lynn Cayce. The drive to Los Angeles could take two or three hours, and we planned to arrive before 10 a.m. so that we might relax a few minutes before our important meeting.

When we knocked at his hotel door, Hugh Lynn welcomed us. His winning smile and warm personality made us feel at ease right away. He was a man of average height, just a little stocky, with a fair complexion and snow-white hair. After we got seated in his room, he smiled and asked, "How can I help you?"

I explained that by education I was an engineer but had been laid off from my job because of lost contracts. For some time, while still employed, I had been giving readings in my spare time. For the past three months, however, I had been giving them for people on a full-time basis, but I was feeling insecure about whether or not they were helpful. When I read through the transcripts, I told him that they didn't always make sense to me. And if I didn't understand them, how could I expect those who received them to be helped? Privately I realized that I was probably looking for an excuse to give up the readings, thereby forcing myself to return to engineering. But of course, I didn't tell Hugh Lynn this.

He listened very carefully. We could see that he was thinking very hard about how he could draw on his own experiences to help us. He had witnessed hundreds—perhaps even thousands—of his father's readings. He had since then investigated dozens of gifted psychics.

First he spoke directly to my concerns that the readings weren't always comprehensible to me. He stated in a kind way that the readings weren't for me, so I shouldn't take it personally if I didn't understand them. That made sense. From that morning on, I began to view the readings in a different light.

Hugh Lynn went on to pose some questions. He wanted to know how I went about doing the readings, and what I found on the other side when I got to the Akashic records. I told him that I would put myself into a deep meditative state and then would leave my body and travel to the place where the records were stored. There, I would meet with my guides and the reading would begin. I described in great detail my visits to the Akashic records. As I talked about the details of my visits, I explained that the floor of the library which I entered wasn't solid, but consisted of what appeared to be clouds; however, I found good support as I walked across the floor. Hearing this, he very thoughtfully replied that his father had often spoken of that same place.

He asked how people requested readings. I told him that they either phoned or wrote for information. Then Doris would send an application form. A soon as it was returned, she scheduled the reading. Hugh Lynn asked about the complexity of the application form, and I explained that it was very simple, requesting only name, address, city, state, and a dated signature. The application stated that a life reading had been requested by the undersigned and that the recipient realized that Doris and I would pray for the person before the reading was taken.

Hearing this, Hugh Lynn suggested that we ask additionally for the birthdate—month, day, and year. Doris asked why that was necessary. He answered that someday in the future we were likely to come across people who have the same first, middle, and last name living in the same city. The only way I'd be able to tell them apart would be by their birthdate. (He was right. Over the years we have come across that situation a number of times.) Unfortunately, when we began requiring the birthdate, a few people cancelled their requests, suggesting that we must be frauds if we had to have the date of their birth.

Then Hugh Lynn questioned us about our office procedures. "How do you maintain order as you store the information from the readings? How do you keep track of those that are yet to be done?" he asked. I didn't understand, so he explained further. "You need to assign a number to each reading. For example, start with #1 for the first reading. You also need to set up a file card for each reading, plus a folder for each completed reading. They should be kept in both an alphabetical and a numerical file. That way you can easily find any reading you may look for when you begin to study and research them."

Then he addressed himself to me and referred to the readings that Doris had sent him. He asked about the identity of my guides. What was my relationship to them from the past? Why were they working with me now? I told him that it had never occurred to me to ask them.

He admonished me sternly and suggested that I had better find out as soon as possible. He cautioned me that these guides may not be honorable and could easily lead me into trouble. He went on to tell me that unless the two guides and I had been working together before, there was no ethical reason why they should show up now. He had an authoritative manner, and I believed he knew what he was talking about. So I promised him that very soon I would do a reading concerning any earlier relationships with the guides. I wanted to clear up that matter.

One other major thing Hugh Lynn touched on was the importance of feedback from those who obtained readings. He suggested we enclose a questionnaire with our scheduling letter. Then the person receiving the reading could answer the questions after listening to the reading and return the form to us. He offered to send us a copy of the questionnaire he had used, saying that we were welcome to use it as is or change it. We gratefully accepted it and didn't change a word. We have used it ever since.

The meeting went on for about an hour. All the while

Hugh Lynn was very supportive, and this encouraged Doris and me in our new work. We knew Hugh Lynn was someone we could turn to again when we needed help. (Later on, when we had the opportunity to visit the A.R.E. headquarters in Virginia Beach several times, Hugh Lynn would always invite us into his office to see how we were doing. These short visits were very meaningful to us.)

As soon as we returned to Santa Maria, we did a reading to find out about my two guides. I met them at the Akashic records and asked them why they felt they had a right to help me. They replied that we had worked together in the past, and now they had been assigned to help me in my present situation. "Where have we been together before and what were we doing?" I asked. I was told that the three of us had been on Mt. Olympus and gave counsel to many souls.

I listened with a skeptical ear. I planned that when I returned to my body I would check up on this information to see if there really was a Mt. Olympus. I was familiar with Mt. Olympus in Greek mythology but had no idea whether or not it actually existed. If I couldn't find such a place, I would return to the Akashic records and request other guides. As it turned out, I found that Mt. Olympus is quite real—a mountain about 150 miles west of Athens in the West Peloponnesus. This reassured me that it was quite appropriate to keep working with these guides.

We also followed Hugh Lynn's advice on our record-keeping. We started to number the readings, made file cards for each of them, and placed the application form and correspondence pertaining to the reading in file folders. I felt better having a system to keep track of the paper work.

As I continued doing readings, I felt a great need to improve the format. Doris had noticed that there wasn't any systematic order to the way the information came through me. In going over her notes, she had recognized that certain subjects kept coming up in the readings, but they came randomly. I wanted the information to be in a dependable format so that people could more easily find specific information in the readings.

Among the subjects that had come up in most readings were past lives, the purpose of incarnating, color vibrations on which the person was born, various factors influencing the individual, colors associated with the spiritual centers at the time of the reading, what the person should do now to accomplish his or her purpose, and the symbol best describing the individual. In addition, there always seemed to be some miscellaneous information that didn't fit any of these categories.

Doris and I talked about the need for a better format one day as we drove to a workshop. We decided that it might be best for all readings to open with a prologue—perhaps the miscellaneous information could go there. The prologue could be universal in scope, or it could specifically address the individual. Next I would describe a symbol that best captured the essential soul characteristics of the particular person. In fact, this element of my readings was proving to be very helpful to recipients. I had discovered after giving readings for about a year that I could obtain a meaningful image for each person, and I could explain its implications for the person's current life situation.

Next, each reading would outline the strongest influences affecting the person—physical, mental, emotional, and spiritual factors. The subsequent topic would be past lives, followed by influential colors. Believing that colors are important, we chose to place this segment directly after the reincarnation information. The last two sections would be the purpose for which the person came into this life and how to accomplish it.

We decided that Doris would bring these distinct elements of the format into focus for each reading by posing them as sequential questions. We both felt better about this format and agreed to try it out when we did our next reading. (Note: See the Appendix for a sample reading in its entirety.)

The weekend retreat to which we were headed proved to be very interesting. It was held in a very large home. Friday evening started with a time of meditation followed by a short prayer. Then I delivered my introductory talk on guidance in daily life. No sooner had I finished and taken my seat when a woman sitting at my left requested that I do a reading for a young man who had accompanied her. She explained that he needed help, and she thought that a reading might give some answers to his difficulties. As it turned out, the woman was Dr. Gina Cerminara, author of several books, including *Many Mansions,* the best seller that explored Edgar Cayce's theories of reincarnation. She hoped that I would honor her request by doing a reading that very evening—since neither of them could come for the Saturday or Sunday meetings.

I had never done a reading in public! There were about fifty people in attendance. To be watched by them—feeling their cross-currents of doubt and skepticism—made me nervous and apprehensive. I wanted to do it, yet I wasn't sure if I should. Doris and I talked it over and agreed to give the reading on just his specific problem and not take time for a complete reading, which would be unfair to the other attendees. This was agreeable to Gina. In a few minutes we were ready to start.

The reading went well, although I wasn't as comfortable as I felt I needed to be to do this work. Apparently the reading was on target. Gina called our host the next day, saying the information from the reading appeared to be very helpful for the young man. While we were happy to have assisted him, Doris and I found it very difficult to do a reading in public. For example, I could feel the different emotions and questions popping up into the minds of the onlookers, and this detracted from the quality of the reading. Since that event we haven't done any public readings.

Having followed through on Hugh Lynn's suggestions, I was beginning to feel more comfortable in my new role. I spent less time looking for a position as an engineer and more time developing and exploring the horizons of the gift that God had given me. That exploration led to some rather unusual frontiers.

Chapter Sixteen
Stretching Ourselves

A t first, the letter seemed like so many others. It was simply a request for a life reading, but this letter would eventually lead me beyond the frontiers of my experience. I would be stretched and challenged to soar past my old horizons.

It all started when a young man from New York wrote that some of his friends had told him about my work. Now he was interested in obtaining a life reading. As usual, Doris sent him our application form. He returned it right away, and Doris scheduled his reading for some four weeks hence—in the middle of May 1972. Jeff Goodman lived across the continent, and other than his name and address, I knew nothing about him.

Shortly after receiving the tape recording of his reading in May, he wrote again. Now he revealed many facts about himself that we hadn't known. He had a degree in geological engineering, a master's degree in business administration, and would soon pursue a doctorate in anthropology. Jeff expressed amazement at what he considered to be the accuracy of his reading, since it included past-life information that clearly pointed to this sort of career path.

What followed was an exchange of letters that led to a stimulating professional relationship and collaboration on a fascinating research project that stretched my psychic abilities.

Jeff requested and received thirty readings in the coming months—readings that focused on the use of psychic information for archaeology. He began by asking where he might excavate on this continent to find evidence of very early civilizations—prior to 100,000 B.C. Three areas were mentioned in the readings—one in Mexico, another in Colorado, and the third in Arizona.

For example, one reading stated, "We find that the area in Colorado—in southern Colorado—and northern Arizona, and also not so much on the East Coast but toward the Gulf of Mexico, which would be the easiest way of finding it. We have pointed out three different areas, the southern Colorado, the northern Arizona, and also the middle part of Arizona, which would be relatively easy, though difficult at times. But there will be skulls, there will be bones, there will be other fossils found near mountains, near the foot of mountains."

Since Jeff planned to attend the University of Arizona that fall to work toward his doctorate, he requested more details on one of the Arizona sites.

This idea of psychic archaeology made me a little nervous. I had never before used my gift in this kind of research. Even though the subject interested me as a scientist, I didn't know if I could help him. Nevertheless, I decided that this was the time to stretch myself beyond old boundaries and to see what I could do. In the end, the results proved to be fascinating.

Before starting on any readings that would give specific archaeological details, I explained to Jeff that he must understand that this was a new area for me. I couldn't promise anything. Jeff agreed that this measure of uncertainty was clear to him, and he chose to concentrate on the potential site near Flagstaff, Arizona. It was close enough to the university that he could excavate for artifacts of an early civilization while working on his doctorate courses on campus in Tucson.

We proceeded to take a reading on the Flagstaff site. It contained great detail, describing the geology and rock formation in that area, the climatic conditions in ancient times, and the types of people who had lived there.

Weeks later another reading gave information as to where to dig in order to find potsherds (pottery fragments) from an ancient civilization. A small dig was proposed as a preliminary effort before attempting any extensive excavation of the site.

With this information in hand, Jeff went to work to test the accuracy of my psychic perception. Doris and I anxiously awaited word. One morning Jeff telephoned from Flagstaff. Excitedly, he explained that he had brought a group of people to the San Francisco Mountains outside Flagstaff and had started to dig in the area which I had indicated in the reading. Sadly, he had found nothing. He was calling from a phone booth at the edge of town and wanted to know what had gone wrong. Snow flurries were in the air, he said, and they were concerned that a storm would blow in before they could find what they were looking for. Time was of the essence.

I asked him to call me back in a couple of hours. In the meantime, I would take a "check reading" to determine the problem. (A check reading is our label for a follow-up reading—usually very short—on the same subject to confirm whether the information from the previous reading needs to be amended.)

After I had finished the scheduled readings for that morning and while I was still in a deep meditation, Doris presented Jeff's problem. She and I had never discussed how to go about doing a check reading for archaeologial purposes. Doris spontaneously decided to try something new. She directed me while I was still in meditation to go to the site where the group was digging and to describe the area. I had no problem projecting myself to the location of the dig. Then Doris instructed me to give an account of everything I saw as I turned in a circle of 360 degrees.

I saw the entire panorama in clear detail. I saw evergreen trees on the right, and on the left there was a dirt road and a dry creek bed. Straight ahead were more trees, and there was a clearing beyond this. The terrain was on an incline and beyond the clearing was a sharp rise. Behind me the landscape went downhill smoothly. Seeing all this, I also realized why Jeff hadn't found the potsherds which were indicated in the previous reading. The group had dug five feet too far south. The check reading gave new directions and said that now they would find what they had come for.

I had no sooner finished the check reading when Jeff called again. Over the phone I played the tape recording of the reading for him. When it was finished, I asked him if the scene I described was anything like the actual dig site as he had seen it. All he said was, "You were there." Then he asked me if I had seen a stake in the ground near where I had been psychically positioned. I told him I hadn't. That seemed to trouble him. At the time I didn't understand the importance of his question. Since there was nothing more to discuss, he hung up and hurried back to the site—a forty-five-minute drive over rough terrain.

A few hours later he called again. With laughter in

his voice he told me he had found the potsherds. He also said that he had solved the mystery of the missing stake. After he had left the site to call me, somebody had removed the stake and put it in the truck, not thinking the marker was any longer important. Jeff had placed the marker there as a possible point of reference for me during the check reading.

With that success and confirmation that the readings had been accurate, Jeff returned to Tucson with plans for the following summer to start a more extensive excavation. He hoped to find numerous artifacts of an early civilization—indisputable evidence that ancient people had lived in that area.

Before the summer project, Jeff invited Doris and me to Tucson that spring. He drove us to the Flagstaff site where we gave another reading. Archaeological information was given in great detail. The reading said what would be uncovered—foot by foot downward—if Jeff were to excavate in that area.

That summer Jeff started the extensive, systematic digging, and the work continued over the next three years. As predicted, he found artifacts. In fifty-five of the fifty-eight cases, the artifacts were in the exact position stated in the readings and at the predicted levels.

Three years later, Jeff's book, *Psychic Archaeology* (Berkley Books, 1977), was published. It presented the detailed story of our research project and its results.

This scientific work with Jeff had been a real eye-opener for me in many ways. Not only did I discover a wider scope to my gift, it also made me deal directly with the skeptical, scientific mindset which a researcher probably needs to have. In the initial stages of our project together, Jeff tested me. Perhaps, at the time, he felt this was necessary to satisfy himself that I would be able to supply the information he was looking for.

For example, once he called and asked me to project myself to his house in Tucson and to provide a description. I was able to find his house more than a thousand miles away and accurately described not only his house but the area where he lived—and at the same time gave him a local weather report. Then good-naturedly, I looked into his storage shed and suggested to him that it could stand to be cleaned up. He later confirmed that I had been right on target.

He had another test for me when we visited him in Arizona in the springtime before the big excavation. When we went to the proposed excavation site in Flagstaff, Jeff announced that he had secretly buried an object about twenty-five feet away from where I was sitting. I went into a light meditation and described it. Afterward he confirmed that I had been accurate. It was a rear left leg-bone of a dog.

Over the years I have grown weary of researchers trying to prove to themselves that the information is valid. But in the beginning, especially with Jeff, it was interesting to discover how far my gift could be developed. I had stretched myself and the information seemed to be helpful.

It was the first of what I have categorized as "research readings," and my curiosity as a scientist was rewarded in the effort. However, it seemed to be a departure from my real goal: to use this gift as a tool to help people with the problems of life. I've done many research readings with others since. Yet I've come to understand that too much focus on testing and research seems like a detour from what I believe was God's intention when He opened this door to me. With that in mind, I have been reluctant to participate in this sort of experimentation because it is physically and mentally draining. Probably for some psychics, such research work is exactly how they are meant to use their talents. But I feel I should expend that energy on helping people through life readings.

Chapter Seventeen
Peeking into the Akasha

Requests for readings were coming in rapidly to our home in Santa Maria, and by midsummer 1971 we were booked for six months in advance. It was about this time that a new element developed in the life readings. In some ways it was an expansion upon the personal *symbol* that had always been a valuable ingredient of each reading. Now this expanded into a *life seal*, largely inspired by the suggestion of a young man who had requested a reading.

He came to visit one afternoon, telling us that his reading was scheduled for early fall and that he had a special request. In his reading he would appreciate information about a personal life seal. He said that people often got descriptions of life seals in readings from Edgar Cayce, and he would like to have one, too.

At first, I wasn't very receptive to the idea. Up to that time, the individual symbol that I gave for each person seemed perfectly adequate. Besides, at that time I didn't even know what a life seal was, so I told him I couldn't promise anything. After he left, Doris and I discussed it. She encouraged me to try to get my own kind of life seal for the young man, not to attempt to copy what Edgar Cayce gave. That's how I'd learn and grow in this work, she suggested. I couldn't argue with her and agreed to make an attempt when his reading came up.

In September 1971 the first life seal came through in his reading. When Doris posed the question to me while I was in a meditative state, I was surprised by the results. I could vividly see images from the Akashic records—a series of symbols arranged in particular positions, with certain colors playing key roles.

I saw and described an hourglass in a wine-red wooden stand. The white sand in the top chamber had only begun to sift through. I intuitively knew the meaning. He was at a new beginning, and I urged him not to allow things to go unfinished or unresolved. There had been tendencies toward overindulgence in his past. Furthermore, he had not fully utilized time. Now he was tending to "observe the parade from the sidelines" when he should be participating instead. He also feared that much of life would pass him by—and that was exactly what was going to happen if he didn't get hold of himself.

I went on in my psychic counsel, still interpreting his life seal. He should establish order in his life, develop plans, set goals, be reluctant to speak but quick to think. I could see that he was in bondage to certain events—situations which, nevertheless, could be for his own gain.

Then I described more of his life seal. Around the hourglass were flowers with deep, blue berries, all of this arranged in an orange circle. Surrounding the circle was a square, and in each corner was an object. In the upper-right corner was an old gangplank from a ship. In the lower-right corner was a gnarled and chipped staff. In the lower-left corner I saw a candle with a tiny flame; in the upper-left, an open eye. These were tied together with a light blue ribbon.

Again, I knew what the images meant and spoke of them as the reading continued. The omniscient, all-seeing eye had always been watching him. He had wanted to go to sea and to live a life of his own liking. The staff symbolized his walking in circles—that is, his difficulties. The candle depicted his inner light. He had been squelching that inner resource. As he would try to live up to his present knowledge and enter the kingdom within, then the candle would glow brighter. The life seal as a whole encouraged him to orient his thinking toward the Spirit of God.

The symbols and colors in his seal were so exciting and inspiring that I decided to obtain a person's life seal from the Akashic records in all future readings. Doris and I realized that the life seal is a symbolic representation of that soul—a richer and more complex picture than can come from a single symbol. Today, when I start a reading and arrive at the Akashic records, I never proceed until I first see the life seal. Sometimes I may observe initially only the central theme in the seal. Then, as I describe that essential part, other symbols begin to appear.

We were so excited about the life seals that we decided to obtain our own. The following is what I got for Doris: Three hands outstretched. All three are like one (that is, one wrist with three hands on it) holding a large amethyst. It's a round, faceted stone which comes to a point at the bottom. This is necessary for her outreach. Surrounding the hands is a yellow circle. On top of the circle is a stepladder for her to ascend. This is her gateway to the kingdom. On the right of the circle there is a scroll, and it's an old medicine book which she used in ancient Egypt. At the bottom of the circle is a torch. The light from within is the light which extends outwardly. On the left of the circle is a path which ends in a great glow and a high spiritual, mental, and physical estate for her.

For my life seal I found two large circles, one inside the other. The inner circle is blue and the outer one is pink. On the right within the inner circle is a thick, open book. That is the book from which my soul has been learning and teaching for many centuries and incarnations. Next to it is a smaller book with small print. This book depicts what my soul has learned. There is much more for me to learn and do.

In the center of the inner circle is a many-faceted diamond indicating persistence, determination, and some sharp edges that still need to be softened. Coming from directly above, a golden light shines into the diamond. Extending out from the diamond are brilliant rays of light in blue, yellow, orange, and various other colors. This image symbolizes decisiveness. To the left of the diamond is a white dove sitting on an olive branch, bringing peace. Below the dove is a globe of the world, and above the globe is inscribed "Go to my people." Below the globe are the words "Bring peace," and on the right "Love all." Finally, on the left is the single word "Forgive." It is the desire of my soul that the people in the world will have a listening ear to the ideas and teachings that come through me. The background of the life seal, beginning at the bottom, is a golden yellow. It fades into a light green and then at the top shifts to blue.

Above the circles are three six-pointed gold stars. In the center of the right star is the word "Peace." In the middle star is "Cooperation," and in the left one is "Balance." Below the circles is a broken, lighted candle. This represents aspirations from past lifetimes where disappointments and frustrations were hidden within.

But now in the present life much activity is bursting forth, both mentally and spiritually. In this lifetime the candle can be repaired through forgiveness and love.

Even though the content and format of the readings have evolved over the years—such as the addition of life seals—the process of doing a reading has remained almost constant. My method for going to the records hasn't changed very much from that first trip. Unlike some other psychics who are in an unconscious trance or self-hypnosis when they do readings, I'm not. Meditation is the vehicle I use to project myself to the records; and not only do I stay fully aware of what I'm doing, I also have a dim awareness of my physical surroundings—at least enough to hear Doris' questions and suggestions. Neither do I allow an entity to speak through me, as do many "channelers." I can't evaluate their method or accuracy. I simply know that's not my way.

I've looked for a biblical basis for what I do. The Old Testament warning against consulting mediums doesn't pertain to my work because no deceased spirits speak through me. The Bible recommends meditation (my principal tool), and I think there are also references to deep altered states of consciousness similar to what I experience. I believe if they are practiced in sincerity, with a focus on God, it can help anyone's spiritual growth. I also believe that the ability to go to the Akashic records is within everyone's reach.

There are many meditation methods, and Doris and I have explored several of them along the way. The simplest form has worked for me. Basically, I believe that prayer and meditation go together. Prayer, it seems to me, is talking to God, while meditation is listening to God.

Doris' presence is a vital part of my ability to give

readings. In a very real sense we are both on a journey in the spirit. Doris' presence is far more than just that of a helper—more than merely someone who can give me information or suggestions. In a very real sense each reading is a product of our combined energy and consciousness. If we are interrupted when I'm doing a reading and Doris must leave the room, that room is suddenly empty. I profoundly feel it. All the energy is just taken out, and I'm helpless until she returns.

An early experience highlighted the necessity of her presence. While still working in the aerospace industry, I was in Boston on business. I had carried with me a letter from a person who needed a reading rather desperately. Being very concerned for him, I decided to do the reading one evening. I noticed that I didn't have the same ease in going to the records, and upon returning I had great difficulty getting back to my body. I really should have known better than to try this without Doris. Since that experience I've always had Doris present when going to the records.

At conferences where we speak about our work, people often want to know what it's like to see the Akashic records—this reservoir of human progress. They also want to know how I obtain the information for which I'm looking. I explain that in my early years of giving readings, I became curious about the Akashic records, too. I had journeyed to that place many times but knew only that it was a library containing information about every soul. I still had no idea what the word "Akashic" meant or for what purpose those records might exist.

In my search through conventional literature, I didn't find very much. I learned that "Akasha" is from the ancient Sanskrit language and means "primary substance." It can also be used to describe principles of life, such as the cycles of birth and death. I also learned that those records are linked with karma, the law of cause and effect—"Whatever you sow, you will also reap."

After failing to find much more information, Doris and I decided to do a reading on the subject, hoping to gain a clearer picture of the role of the Akashic records in our lives. According to that reading, the Akasha are records where all souls who have passed from the physical into the nonphysical have deposited an imprint of all their life experiences. It's a collection place to which souls can return in order to have the opportunity to go over their own lives, the most recent incarnation, or farther back. From this sort of review, souls can learn and recognize where the pitfalls have been, as well as successes they have achieved. This reading said:

It is here where the individual will look, usually after death, into his own records. In other words, it is a time to review, a time to re-evaluate, a time to learn from mistakes and accomplishments. The intent is to recognize the karmic situations and consider how they may be resolved. Obviously, this is an important step in the growth of a soul.

It seems that each soul may also review its own records with a purpose of obtaining a broader view of the actions or activities that are of concern. The soul may then have the opportunity to learn about its limitations, weaknesses, strengths, or whatever else is needed to build a person with substance and integrated character.

Before a soul enters into another incarnation that soul will again review its own records to keep fresh in its mind the purpose for re-entering the earth plane.

When the soul then enters the earth for another life experience, there is always the quiet voice of
God from within to give direction for choices and
behavior. If the soul listens to that quiet voice, the
message is there, and all that is needed is to act
upon it. (Reading #R10-18)

I have always thought it curious that when I do a
reading, I see the Akashic records as a modern-day
library, filled with large books placed on huge shelves.
Each book contains information written by an expert
calligrapher. If the Akashic records are millions of years
old, why does the information appear to me in a
modern-day format?

I suppose, if I had been born in a culture where clay
tablets were used I would see the information on clay
tablets. The same would be true if I lived in a culture
where scrolls were used or any other method for com-
piling information. I came to understand that I would
see the records in the form to which I was accustomed.
With the computer age upon us, someone else traveling to the Akashic records might very well see the
information on a monitor. In essence a person per-
ceives the Akashic records by whatever form is familiar
to him or her.

On one of my trips to the Akashic records, my guides
handed me a plastic card, with instructions that I
would know how to use it inside the library. Once inside, instead of looking through the books of life, I
found myself sitting in a large chair, facing a huge
screen. I inserted the plastic card into a slot in the left
armrest. Immediately, the information I was seeking
appeared on the monitor. All I needed to do was to
watch the events as they appeared and to relay the
information. On subsequent trips to the Akasha, how-

ever, I resumed my usual method of obtaining the large books from the shelves and going through them for information.

Sometime later, I used another method for obtaining information about past lives. After going through the records, I projected myself back through time to the particular lifetimes where the experiences shown in the records took place. From that vantage point, I observed the person's behavior and even felt very strongly his or her emotions, attitudes, and thought processes. Since 1971 when I discovered I could do this, I've followed this method ever since.

About three years after my initial experience at the Akasha, as I started to give a reading and came to the familiar fork in the road, I kept going straight ahead instead of my usual left turn. I felt that it was time to explore this alternate path. It brought me to the same temple from a different approach. I had always assumed that where I entered was the front door; however, looking at the temple from this new viewpoint, I realized that I hadn't been seeing the main entrance, but instead a side door.

Now, directly in front of me was a long, narrow stairway made from pure white marble and lined on both sides with rose bushes. As usual, it was very quiet. I climbed the stairway. At the top I met two guides—not my usual ones. They greeted me and explained that they would be my new guides. One was a Chinese gentleman and the other a Greek. The Chinese man wore a black skullcap with a pigtail showing down his back. He wore a black silk, hand-embroidered kimono. The Greek guide wore a short white toga.

The Chinese guide took charge and explained the new routine I was to follow. Whenever I came to the records, I would present myself to them before entering the main library. "We will give you some advice, when needed, each time you come here," he said. "But for the most part you are now on your own." I was told, very precisely, that I would be observed and corrected if I encountered trouble. They wouldn't go with me into the library to search for information. They would remain on the outside, available if I needed help. I was also cautioned that just because I was now being allowed to enter through the main entrance, I shouldn't become prideful or high-minded about it.

In fact, a series of events led up to my decision not to take my usual left turn on the pathway. Over the years I have had several sets of guides. As I've described, the first time I arrived at the records, my two guides were waiting for me. They escorted me into the library and did all the work for me. After that, each time I came to the records these same guides told me what to look for in the books as they watched closely over my shoulder. I was corrected on a number of occasions, and I learned to be more careful and accurate. Then, one day my guides said they were leaving. They had been transferred to some other place where they could teach someone else.

Knowing this, I wasn't surprised when the next day I arrived at the records to find another set of guides. I asked them what had happened to my first set and the account of their being transferred was confirmed. My second set of guides taught me how to interpret symbols and colors. As with my first set of guides, following Hugh Lynn's advice, I challenged these guides with: "Do you come in the name of Jesus Christ? And do you believe that He has come in the flesh?" The answer was yes to both questions.

The course of instruction lasted several months. Every day I met with them. They showed me how to interpret symbols and taught me the meaning of colors in connection with the symbols. Day after day I retraced my steps to the records, met my two guides, and the instruction would continue as I obtained information for that reading.

One day a year later when I arrived at the records, I noticed my guides were troubled. I asked them why, and they told me that they, too, were being reassigned to another part of the Akasha. The next day I made my decision to forego my usual left turn at the fork and subsequently found the staircase flanked with roses and the true front door. Since then I've been on my own, so to speak. At first I felt a bit apprehensive, but I mustered courage, knowing what good tutoring I had received. I was determined to apply all I had learned.

Over the years it's been important to me to get feedback from recipients of my readings. Confirmation of their accuracy and helpfulness has come from positive, encouraging letters and from phone calls I've received from those who obtained readings. Without that I could have easily lost confidence in this work and would have probably given it up—as I almost did after a woman from the East Coast challenged the validity of her reading.

In her request for a reading, she wrote about an unusual episode. On a visit to a Williamsburg cemetery, she stopped to read the gravestone of a person named Katherine Thorp. She explained that she had become very emotional and for no apparent reason broke out in uncontrollable sobbing. She wondered why she had experienced such an outburst, and she asked if a reading might help her learn if she could possibly have been connected in some way to the woman who was buried there.

When I went to the Akashic records for her reading, I found some fascinating information. I discovered that she had been Katherine Thorp, living in Williamsburg in the 1600s and was the wife of a seafarer. She had died from a disease in her early 40s. I saw her as a small, frail woman, and the hardships had overtaken her. Of course, she didn't want to die and fought it with the little strength she had. To leave her children alone broke her heart. I explained to the one requesting the reading that when she came upon the tombstone, the emotion from this past life overtook her.

A week after we mailed the cassette tape of the reading, she called us. She was very disappointed, saying that not only had I been wrong many times in the reading, but I also had gotten the information on the grave marker wrong. She stated emphatically that the gravestone said "never married," and the word "relic" was also inscribed. That call shattered my confidence.

Afterward Doris and I went for a walk. As we talked, I contended that if my information was that inaccurate, I shouldn't continue to do readings any longer. The last thing I wanted to do was to mislead people. Doris agreed.

Coming back to the house, she suggested that before making any drastic decision we first do a little checking on our own. So we wrote to the office of the county recorder in Williamsburg, Virginia, and requested information about Katherine Thorp. Ten days later we heard from the county clerk. She wrote, "Most of our records prior to 1865 have been either lost or destroyed by fire. The few remaining ones are in Virginia State Library." She referred us to the Archives Division, Virginia State Library in Richmond, Virginia. She also suggested that we write to the Virginia Historical Society.

Following her advice, we sent a letter to the Virginia State Library, explaining that we were seeking information about a Katherine Thorp, who we believe lived in the 1600s and who is buried in a cemetery in Williamsburg. We also asked if they might shed some light on the word "relic" inscribed on her tombstone.

While waiting, I continued doing readings. But in my mind I knew that the answer from Virginia State Library would determine whether or not I would stay with this work.

A few weeks later we heard from the Library. They didn't have much information but offered to send a photocopy of the inscription on the grave marker and the official record of Bruton Parish Church regarding Katherine Thorp. They also explained that the word "relic" had either been misread or weathered beyond recognition. The word was actually "relict," which meant "widow." They also explained that the epitaph didn't contain the words "never married."

This information renewed my confidence. It demonstrated that I was able to pick up accurately facts about the distant past with my psychic awareness. I was at peace with my work.

At times, however, the information given in a reading doesn't seem to have any particular relevance to the one for whom it is intended—relevance at least at the time the individual first hears it. Sometimes only months or *years* later does it begin to make sense. That was the case with a schoolteacher, Lee Ashton, who listened to her tape-recorded reading for a second time after eight years. This schoolteacher had just attended an A.R.E. conference at which one of the speakers, Dr. Harmon Bro, had mentioned our work. Later, she wrote a letter to Dr. Bro telling him how the conference had helped her and how the reference to our readings had sparked a search for the one she had long ago obtained.

She wrote, "The tape was at home in a box of little-remembered psychic, harp, astrological, and numerological readings from my more phenomenon-oriented spiritual stage. When I got home, I went searching for the tape and settled into my bed to listen again, after eight years, to a tape I had deemed too boring and convoluted to deal with. I had never even listened to the entire tape. A few minutes into the tape, I sat bolt up in bed. Wow! There was the answer to my decade of unrest."

She explained that in 1979 when the reading was done, her goal was to work with the terminally ill—especially children. As she wrote to Dr. Bro, "I had heard about Abrahamsen and gotten his address from a friend at Virginia Beach. I wrote and asked for a reading. I waited a long time, but finally it came. I was very disappointed when I listened to the first part because it made not one wit of sense to me. I was not even thinking in the direction it was suggesting. I didn't know what in the world had happened—had he got me mixed up with someone else?

"He was talking about my mission in life being involved with the soil, and he told me to look into something called *hydroponics.* I just ignored it."

Her letter went on to detail years of trying to follow her intended field, but being side-tracked time and time again. These so-called detours took her through a myriad of experiences: teaching science, gardening pursuits, alternative habitats. Finally her interests peaked in earth science and hydroponics—the science of growing plants in liquid solutions (instead of soil) containing the necessary minerals. Suddenly doors began opening. After having gone through so many frustrating digressions from her original interests, the success in this new field almost frightened her.

"Now, in the throes of self-doubt, terrified of success, I began again to search for purpose," she explained to Dr. Bro. "My ego was so involved and so screwed up that at the point at which I drove to the conference I was on the edge of suicide. But I came to your sessions seeking a word or a phrase that would put me in touch with my purpose. When it came, I didn't recognize it. When I applied it later, I was shocked at how blind I had been to it all these years.

"Listening to that [Abrahamsen] tape affirmed that I am actually moving toward what I am supposed to do in this life. A calm has come over me that I have not known for a very long time. I have no idea where it will lead."

Naturally, Doris and I were deeply gratified when Dr. Bro shared this letter with us. It's reports like this one that offer Doris and me our special rewards. They reinforce the decision we made those many years ago to help people by giving the readings. So often we've seen a principle: although the recipient may be unaware of it at the time of the reading, the message contained in his or her reading is very personal and individual. I remain confident that the information I get from the Akashic records deals specifically with the person's mission. Often it answers a cry for help.

Requests for readings come in a variety of ways. We may receive a phone call or letter saying, "A friend of mine got a reading, and I'd like to have one, too." Many inquiries came after we were listed in a register of psychics in Dr. William Kautz's book, *Channeling: The Intuitive Connection.* We didn't even know the book had been published until we started getting calls. In 1974 Dr. Kautz had been impressed by his reading and helped spread the word through the book. I'm thankful that throughout the years we've been doing readings all promotion has been by word of mouth. We've never felt the need to commercialize ourselves or promote our work. We feel that God will move those who need a reading to contact us.

In all that time—twenty-two years now—we've always had a backlog of requests. In fact, at one time the demand was so great that I scheduled fifteen readings a week. But then I got a warning from my guides. I had gone to the records as usual and was ready to begin a reading when one of my guides stopped me. He said very definitely that if I didn't slow down my reading schedule, I would be on a collision course in five years. I took that to mean that in five years I might not be around anymore. After that reading concluded, I told Doris what my guide had said. That very day we decided that all future requests would have to fit into a much less-demanding schedule. But that change would have to wait—we were already scheduled two years ahead, and I felt that it was crucial to keep those commitments.

In the meantime, Doris and I knew that our time in Santa Maria was nearing its end. We remembered clearly the one very important reading that had described our destiny. We were going to be relocating to southern Oregon, so we started preparing for the move.

It wasn't Doris and I alone who considered making such a move. At a sharing meeting in Santa Maria, we had met David and Gladys Harper, who took an interest in our work. We told them that we wouldn't be living in Santa Maria for much longer, according to our guidance from a reading. We were to move to Oregon—around the Medford area. That interested them since they had been considering a move to that same area.

Over the next few months we became close friends and together made plans for the four of us to relocate. Among our discussions was the possibility of establishing a spiritual retreat center in that area. We decided that the four of us would work together to make that dream come true.

Chapter Eighteen
The Oregon Adventure

L
ike its majestic mountain peaks and lush, pri-
meval valleys, our Oregon experience was to
be filled with emotional highs and lows. In
those three-and-one-half years, Doris and I were to
experience some of our greatest rewards since entering the field of psychic counseling. We also would
weather some of our greatest disappointments. It was
to be a time of maturing and settling comfortably into
our work, a time of spiritual growth. In 1971, as our
time in California drew to a close, something in us
seemed to know that Oregon would be a wonderful
opportunity. As we prepared ourselves for the move,
we stepped out into this unknown land with high
hopes and a dream.

The Harpers moved on ahead of us. Upon getting
settled, they started looking for property where we
could all live and start the spiritual retreat center. The
arrangement was that Doris and I would continue with
the readings, plus conduct retreats and conferences.
They would operate the business side of the center and
have the responsibility of whatever the property might
require. Doris and I had been to Oregon twice to look
for property but hadn't found anything we believed to

be suitable. It wasn't too long before the Harpers called us, asking for specific guidance about where they should look for property. We took a reading and learned that the property should be near trees and water, situated southwest of Medford.

A week later they called again. They had found forty acres with a large farmhouse and big barn. The property bordered on a forest and extended into the middle of the Applegate River. It certainly sounded as if they had found the place indicated by the reading. They wanted us to come up as soon as possible to see it. A few days later Doris and I flew to Medford. Indeed, it appeared to be what I had envisioned in the reading. It was agreed among the four of us that by pooling our resources we could purchase the property.

Upon our return to Santa Maria, Doris and I started to pack. On December 30, 1971, we left California and began this new phase of our lives. We left family and friends and started our journey to Oregon.

We arrived in Applegate and moved into the large farmhouse with the Harpers until we could build a house for ourselves. Our friends and new partners had collected our mail while we were en route, and there was lots waiting. The next day while relaxing and resting from the trip, we sifted through the letters—all requests for readings. In the days that followed, we answered those letters, but more and more mail arrived. The requests for readings were really piling up.

Doris and I were eager to begin work preparing the place to be a retreat center. We wondered if the big barn could be remodeled and turned into a conference center. It had room for a good-sized kitchen, dining room, and meeting hall, plus a number of sleeping rooms. Using our imagination, we began to see the possibilities. We talked it over with the Harpers and we all agreed that remodeling the barn was the proper way to proceed. But this would have to wait until the finances were available.

I thought that as long as we were going to have a conference center, why not use it for a school, too? It would be a place where people could learn how to cope better with a world of pain and sorrow. I would call it a School of Living. The curriculum could include spiritual principles, creativity, the secular and religious history of the world, elements of music and color, healing, prayer, and meditation.

In the meantime, Doris and I were busy with the readings. Soon we were into a steady rhythm, still at fifteen per week. In February, in addition to the regularly scheduled life readings, I gave the first research reading on color. This was soon followed by readings on music and color healing. These research readings produced an extraordinary amount of information. It seemed so important that we transcribed those readings and kept them in our files. At first we didn't know what we were going to do with them, but we hoped that someday we might have an opportunity to experiment with these innovative methods of healing.

During this period we also relied heavily on guidance from the readings for decisions about our work. We asked questions about dealing with the management of the property, cooperation among those on the land, and the attitudes to be developed. In addition to this rigorous schedule of readings, I also conducted a Bible class and prayer group once a week. We had become very busy and soon discovered that we could use some help.

Fortunately, a family moved into our area and took an interest in our work. Sandra, the mother of two school-age children, offered her services. She made a wonderful administrative assistant, taking a lot of the burden of running the office from Doris and me.

Once we had that help, Doris and I were able to turn our attention to building a new house on the property. We hired a local contractor, and in three months the house was finished. It was up on the mountainside overlooking the Applegate Valley. It was truly a home in which Doris and I could enjoy peace and serenity.

By the spring of 1973, two more families moved near us because of their interest in our work, which meant that two additional gracious women volunteered to help in our office. With the help of these three wonderful ladies everything ran smoothly in the office.

For many months Doris and I had discussed the responsibility we felt to make information available to more people. We could see tremendous possibilities from sharing with a wider audience the ideas and principles in the readings. We decided to establish an organization whereby material from the readings could be shared with the members. We called it Association for the Integration of Man (A.I.M.). We chose the word "Integration" because the readings emphasized so often the importance of balancing and integrating body, mind, and spirit. From our mailing list of those who had received readings, we invited anyone who wished an opportunity to join the Association to do so for a nominal annual fee.

Through a quarterly packet, each member received information on Bible study plus material from the readings in five categories: integration, the kingdom of God, earth changes, ancient civilization, and music and color. As new material became available, new sections were added.

While not overwhelming, the response was sufficient for us to know that there was genuine interest. Doris and I began selecting excerpts from the readings and arranged particularly helpful passages into the categories. Every day after we had finished the scheduled readings, I would spend the rest of the day sorting through material. It wasn't just I who was kept busy. Doris and all our volunteers were very active with plans for the retreat center and the launching of A.I.M.

Unfortunately, by early 1973 we were facing a financial crisis. For some time Doris and I had realized that the donations we received for readings weren't sufficient to meet our basic needs. Even though we were booked ahead for two years, it was a struggle to spread the money far enough to pay our bills. I didn't feel it was right to set a fee for the readings, and Doris agreed. The information came from God, after all, so why should there be a charge for it? I had struggled with that problem since the beginning, but as yet I hadn't found an answer.

Then one day Floyd and Bev Hewett, who lived in Portland, Oregon, came for a visit. We had been friends for several years, and Floyd was a very successful businessman. During dinner he asked me how things were going. I told him, in a guarded way, that it was fine. He sensed that I wasn't telling the whole truth. He knew that we weren't charging for the readings and said that we had to set a minimum fee. Doris and I tried to explain carefully our hesitation—what he was proposing just didn't seem like the right thing to do. But Floyd reasoned that people had no idea about our needs and could only guess how much to include as a donation. In fact, many sent nothing. Floyd kept trying to convince us that setting a fee was the proper and moral thing to do.

The discussion continued as we tried to air all points of view. I countered with, "But this is *spiritual* work.

How can anyone put a price on that?"

Bev responded, "Everything I do honestly and with integrity is spiritual—even scrubbing out garbage cans, cleaning bathrooms, as well as praying for people. Keep in mind that your real identity is Spirit. You live in a physical body and are trying to cope in a material world. Don't be afraid to ask for a fee. The Bible says that the servant is worthy of his hire."

By the time Floyd and Bev left, Doris and I had come to the conclusion that we must follow their advice. The next day we got busy mailing out notices to everybody who had readings scheduled. The letter told them of our change in policy. The suggested contribution would be $50.00 (although the fee increased in later years).

Almost immediately we received answers; some included a check. There were many who didn't respond at all. However, there were a few who called us frauds and canceled their requests for readings. It was difficult for us to have to set a fee, and it hurt to be called frauds. But we knew that if we were to continue in this work, we at least had to have our basic needs met. We also knew we weren't frauds, so we forgave in our hearts those who said we were.

After rescheduling the readings for those who still wanted them, our backlog was reduced to only six months. I felt much more comfortable with that schedule, remembering the warning that my guide gave concerning the workload. In the rescheduling we kept the number of readings to only ten a week.

Peace had now settled over the work, and I was quite happy with it. Nevertheless, every summer, for some reason I had the strong urge to return to engineering. I would buy the *Los Angeles Times* and look through the want-ads for openings in my field. This urge kept resurfacing for many summers until I finally gave up ever returning to engineering and settled down for good to do the readings.

One day Maria DeRungs, a professional musician and professor of music, came to visit. She said that a mutual friend had told her that we had done readings on music therapy. We confirmed her information, explaining that we had done a series of readings on music and color but hadn't had the time to do anything with it. She was immediately interested and asked if she could see some of the transcripts.

After studying through these research readings, she volunteered to compile the information into a booklet. Since she was performing that summer at a nearby music festival, she could come several times a week to start the compilation. Doris and I were immediately taken by her and enthusiastically accepted her offer. Throughout that summer we looked forward to her visits because she was so delightful. She wore her dark hair short, her eyes sparkled, and there was a constant smile on her face. Although she was of fragile appearance, she was still full of energy. Whenever she walked around the office to look for material, she was almost running, as if she were in a hurry. There was so much for her to do in a very short time, since she had taken a teaching and performing position at a college in Kentucky. In fact, she began teaching in her classes the principles from that booklet from that time on.

The following year we received the completed manuscript. We published it under the title: "Attunement of Body, Soul, and Spirit Through Music and Color." Later, Maria DeRungs opened a research center in Everett, Washington, for music and color therapy using the readings as a basis. She calls it Casa de Maria Music Center. Her research there has included some remarkable success.

For example, one of her clients, a twenty-six-year-old named Judith, had Hodgkin's disease. She had refused medicine and chemotherapy treatment. From November 28, 1984, to March 21, 1985, she had weekly sessions consisting of music from Bach, Beethoven, Chopin, and Mendelssohn, with various colored lights appropriate for the music. Before the first music therapy session, her white blood cell count far outbalanced the red cell count. Her blood pressure was very low, and the lymphatics exhibited blockages. There were difficulties in her nervous and glandular systems. At the conclusion of her last session, all her difficulties had been cleared up, with the result that her skin color was better, her swollen liver was reduced, the film over her eyes had disappeared, her sleep patterns and temperature had stabilized, and the digestive system was greatly improved.

According to our research readings on music healing, here is what was taking place. The music from Bach helped repair the overall neurological system, making it more in harmony with the brain function. Beethoven's compositions worked with the mental processes and the energy field to re-establish harmony. The vibrations from Chopin's music worked to unblock the lymphatic and glandular systems. Mendelssohn's music worked on the energy system of the heart, allowing the healing to be regenerated throughout the body.

Maria DeRung's booklet entitled "The Healing Tones of Music" describes the experiences with her clients. We urged her to use the information from our readings and then to move on from there, developing her own intuition for her work. She has done this, and her therapy has proven to be very successful.

In contrast, we weren't going so well as far as the

retreat center was concerned. Unfortunately, the Harpers who had wanted to help us develop the center, started expressing dissatisfaction with the arrangements that involved them taking responsibility for the management of the land. Before too long, serious conflicts arose and the entire project had to be shelved. Had Doris and I sought God's guidance more directly on the retreat center—as we had in all other ventures—we may not have taken this detour. In the past we had always prayed and then found that doors would be opened for new projects. But in this case, it had seemed like such a good idea to our personal, conscious selves that we were convinced it must be part of God's will for our work. It felt as if it just had to be. But it wasn't. Even though we have grown spiritually in the years thereafter, this failure still nags at my soul. Since entering the work of psychic counseling full time, that experience stands as one of only two dark clouds in an otherwise cloudless sky. The second would soon come.

When it was obvious that the development of the retreat center project was bogged down, Doris and I found an alternative way to do at least some of the educational work. We organized a series of weekend conferences at a hotel in Medford. To share the spiritual truths that we have learned through our spiritual evolution has always been an important part of our work.

We had faced the disappointment of seeing our dreams of a spiritual retreat center and School of Living fade away like the fog lifting over the Applegate Valley on a summer morning. Doris and I decided it was time to start preparing for our next move, which had been promised in the readings. We looked northward toward Washington and put our beautiful home in Applegate Valley up for sale.

While waiting for the property to sell, we had the opportunity to work with Jeff Goodman again. For some time Doris and I had been concerned about earth changes and the dire predictions given by a number of people. While living in California, we had also been aware of many families leaving the state because of the predicted earthquakes. We decided to take some readings on earth changes.

Although I had been trained as an engineer, geology and the science of plate tectonics were foreign to me. From experience I had found that to obtain good answers in a reading, the questions needed three features. They had to be intelligently posed, they needed a purpose behind them, and they had to be directed with insight by the questioner. I didn't know anybody who had technical knowledge on this subject except Jeff Goodman.

Doris and I called Jeff and explained our desire to do research readings on earth changes. We admitted that we didn't know enough about the subject to ask intelligent questions. To our surprise and delight Jeff offered to come to Medford and stay with us until the readings were finished. He said he would work on the questions beforehand so that he would be well prepared. We arranged a time when he would be free to travel.

We met Jeff at the Medford airport, and I helped him with his luggage. One suitcase in particular was very heavy, and I asked if he were carrying rocks from Arizona. He smiled and said, "Not quite." After Jeff settled into our guest room, I learned that he had brought a virtual library of books on geology and plate tectonics, plus a whole series of geological maps. He certainly came well prepared.

Jeff was a very energetic young man. He had knowledge in a number of scientific fields, tempered with a good sense of humor. It was intellectually stimulating and a joy to have him in our home. It seemed to me as if there wasn't anything in the fields of science, business, history or politics that he hadn't studied. True to his nature, when he became interested in some subject, he was never satisfied until he had become an expert. I think he succeeded in whatever he undertook.

Jeff was very likeable. Being with him again reminded me of our first time with him years ago. I had felt an immediate rapport. What's more, my respect and admiration for him grew during the time of these earth change readings.

Before we started doing the readings, Jeff explained the plan he felt we should follow to make sure every point was covered. He was very methodical and I appreciated that.

Every morning after finishing our regularly scheduled life readings, the three of us started on the earth changes readings. I would quiet myself, close my eyes, and meditate until the information started to come. Each reading took from one to two hours, and Jeff would ask the questions — sometimes in several different ways to make sure I understood the query and that he understood the response. Often, he would fold out one of his many maps, putting it on the floor and asking questions while he was studying these charts. Once, I remember, he put his finger on an area of the map and asked a question about that region. I, being out-of-body, suggested he move his finger down the map to another spot where more activity in the earth could be anticipated. Later, he told me that he marveled at how, with my eyes closed, I knew where he should move his finger. I couldn't explain it either. I was out of my body and just knew.

After each session, the reading was transcribed and copies were made—one for our files and one for Jeff. By the end of two weeks, we had completed the series, and Jeff returned to his home in Tucson. Later, he incorporated some of this material into his book, *We Are the Earthquake Generation*.

This was the last time that we worked with Jeff. Regretfully, a friction between us arose over the proprietary ownership of these readings, and it resulted in a rift in our relationship. This was the second dark cloud in our long experience with this psychic work. Jeff's participation in our work brought about some of the more fascinating and interesting facets of my psychic gift, and his contribution to this development was undeniable. Looking back, I wish that this conflict could have been avoided because Doris and I lost not only an important and stimulating collaborator, but an exceptionally good friend. We count this loss among our greatest disappointments.

In the summer of 1974 we finally had an interested buyer for our home. As soon as the preliminary papers were signed, Doris and I drove to Washington, and our first stop was North Seattle. After a quick look around, we decided that the area was too noisy and busy, so we headed farther north and came to Everett. It looked peaceful. It was small, and it was on the shores of Puget Sound. The baskets of flowers hanging from the lamp posts added to the town's charm. We felt comfortable here. So we contacted a realtor, and he showed us several new homes. After sifting through the possibilities, we made our choice and presented an offer, contingent upon the sale of our house in Applegate. Then, we asked him how to get to the beach. It was wonderful to discover that we were only ten minutes away.

We drove out through a beautiful tree-lined boulevard. As it curved its way to the beach, we saw glimpses of the water. We drove right to the water's edge, parked the car, and walked around. It was a sunny Sunday afternoon, and the beach was alive with activity—families picnicked on the lawn, boats cut their way through the blue water, and children's laughter filled the air. Doris and I stood with tears welling up in our eyes. It was like coming home. We had found the place we wanted to live, and on the way back to our motel we thanked God for having brought us here.

When we returned to Applegate, we started to pack, anticipating a move within forty-five days. But it wasn't to be. The potential buyers of our property changed their minds. Another disappointment. But then I remembered Psalm 37:23: "The steps of a good man are ordered by the Lord," and playfully someone had once added, "and so are the stops."

I notified the realtor in Everett that we had to cancel our transaction and told him we would be back when our property actually sold. We wondered why God had stopped us so abruptly when everything seemed to be going so smoothly. But I was sure there was a reason.

There was nothing else to do but to continue with the readings in Applegate and work on material for A.I.M. members. All the while Doris and I longed to leave the area.

It was during this lull between moves that I received a request for a reading from Dr. William Kautz, an engineer at Stanford Research Institute. After he received his reading, he shared it with Minoru Kodera, the Institute's Japanese representative in Tokyo. This initiated a new aspect of service for our work—an international outreach for our readings.

Shortly afterward, we received a request for a reading from Minoru. He was very impresseed with the information that came in his reading, and he began recommending us to his friends and associates. It resulted in an avalanche of requests for readings from Japan. For several years thereafter, six out of ten readings were for people in Japan. It's fascinating to me that I'm probably better known in Japan than in the United States. This fact is particularly ironic when I think back on the resentment I held for the Japanese people prior to my experience of healing those soul memories. Through the years Doris and I have become good friends with Minoru, and today he remains our liaison for Japan. His role is vital since he translates each reading from English to Japanese.

A year went by before we finally received another bid for our house in Applegate. This time the transaction went through. In Everett, we renewed our search for a new home with a lady from the same real estate office we had used previously. The house that we liked before was no longer on the market, so we spent three days looking at property, but nothing we saw suited us.

On the morning of the fourth day the realtor stopped at a house that had just come on the market. Even though she presumed that it wouldn't suit our needs, she wanted to see it because it might fit another client. It would take her only a minute, she explained.

Upon arriving, I asked if we could come in and look around, too, while she was checking it out. As soon as Doris and I had seen both floors, we knew this was it. Remembering the words of the realtor—"It has just come on the market"—I now knew why God had stopped us a year earlier from buying a house. We knew in our hearts that this was going to be our new home. The realtor was astounded when I told her we'd like to make an offer on the house right then.

Doris and I signed the papers and within the hour were en route back to Oregon. On Friday, July 11, 1975, the moving van loaded our belongings and departed for Everett. Doris and I left the next day and two days later arrived at the new house.

It was good to be home.

Our sojourn in Oregon had been good in many ways and disappointing in others. Yet, Doris and I were confident that it was part of God's plan, and the disappointments were an ordeal of fire. Like tempered steel, we were now ready to face the promise of the next phase of our lives.

CHAPTER NINETEEN
COMING HOME

Harmony and peace once again returned to our lives. Within a few months our troubles and disappointments from Oregon were but distant memories. In fact, a few years later we visited close friends in the Applegate Valley, and we drove past our former home. Looking up on the hill, we were stunned to see that the house had burned to the ground, leaving hardly a trace. (Fortunately, we learned, no one was hurt in the fire.) It was as though we had never lived there. We were on our own and independent once again. Doris and I felt enriched and revitalized in spirit as the possibilities of life in Washington began to unfold.

The panoramic view from our living room overlooked the city of Everett and beyond to the Cascades. On clear days—and there were many—the mountains stood in sharp silhouette against the sky-blue background. We could smell the alluring aroma of the waters of nearby Puget Sound. Surely, we had the best of everything and thanked God that He had led us once again in a sure and safe way. We settled in to continue our work.

Our new home was a split-level design. We lived upstairs and used the lower floor for offices. We selected one of the spare upstairs bedrooms for the area where we would conduct the readings. We threw ourselves into the readings with rejuvenated energy and enthusiasm.

After establishing our daily routine, Doris and I turned our attention to an aspiration that had thus far eluded us. Over the years people from across the country who had received readings and knew of our work inquired whether or not we might be speaking in their areas. They wanted to meet us, and Doris and I wanted to meet them, too. We decided that the time was now right to make plans for a speaking tour around the country.

Initially, we didn't realize how big an undertaking it was going be. Our plan was to drive, so we bought a new station wagon to ensure that we wouldn't have car problems on the way. The entire tour would take about three months. We mapped out our itinerary, arranged for a contact person in each city where we intended to stop, and outlined the various programs in detail. Our schedule called for all-day meetings on weekends. During the week there would be evening gatherings.

We considered all anticipated expenses. The meetings would bring in a little income and that would help defray some expenses, but more was needed. It became obvious that we didn't have the resources necessary unless we could continue to do our readings along the way.

A friend who had years of experience organizing and planning tours detailed a fifteen-page checklist for us which would make the tour a pleasant experience— and one without surprises. We followed it, and it worked very well.

In the spring of 1976 we embarked upon this new adventure. We had packed all the reading requests that we planned to do along the way, as well as the administrative materials—tapes, envelopes, and stamps for mailing the tapes. The back of our station wagon looked like a small office. As I glanced at the loaded vehicle, I imagined that had there been room for the kitchen sink we probably would have taken that along, too.

Our tour started with speaking engagements in Oregon and down the coast of California. This was an exciting time for Doris and me, and we treasured the chance to make new friends and finally meet our supporters—people who knew us only from the readings we had given. As we expected, there were many chances for us to grow spiritually—and even unexpected opportunities.

In Walnut Creek, California, we learned that it hadn't rained for over a year, and the people at the meeting were very worried about the ramifications of the continuing drought. I noticed the concern on their faces as they spoke about it. Doris and I got together to confer over lunch and decided to make a slight change in our program. We would bring to their attention the enormous benefit of "toning." Years earlier while living in Redlands, we had learned this technique. Toning itself, as explained by Laurel Elizabeth Keyes in her book *Toning, the Creative Power of the Voice,* is nothing more than sound vibration set up by our voices—but vibrations that can have extraordinary effects. In some ways toning is similar to chanting, but in this case the word which is used is directly related to the immediate need.

That afternoon we explained to the program participants that we had used toning for some time with amazing success. It had been utilized, we continued, for financial difficulties, sickness, painful relationships, and—yes—the weather.

Doris suggested that if the participants desired, they could tone for rain to see how it worked. The group enthusiastically agreed to try it as an experiment. Doris gave the instructions, and I hummed the note on which to tone. The whole group toned on the word "rain." All of us could feel the unity, harmony, and oneness of purpose during the toning session. Afterward we took a break. Most of those at the conference went to the door to see if there were any clouds in the sky which might indicate rain. There were none.

I urged them not to be discouraged—to give God something with which to work and allow a little time for it to happen. Later that afternoon clouds started forming—but still no rain.

All during the week that followed, at other meetings along the coast, each group experimented and toned for rain. The following weekend we had a meeting in Santa Barbara, and it rained so much that we were afraid there would be a flood. I concluded that the toning from each group had followed us all the way to Santa Barbara.

Our schedule was often grueling. Usually we would arrive at our destination in time for dinner. There would be a meeting from 8:00 to 10:00 p.m. It was typically 11:00 by the time we got to bed. Doris would set the alarm for 2 a.m., and we would get up to do a psychic reading. We would return to bed about an hour and a half later. By 7:00 in the morning, we were on our way to the next stop.

It was a thrill for us to meet our friends face to face, and every meeting was an exhilarating experience. Our schedule of meetings took us through Arizona, Texas,

Arkansas, Kentucky, and along the east coast to Maine. Then we moved westward to Toronto, Detroit, and Milwaukee. All this time the readings were being done in the middle of the night. More than likely, we were driving ourselves too hard because in Milwaukee fate intervened.

The schedule called for three consecutive evening seminars there. During the day we were free to rest, and we needed it because we were truly exhausted. That first night in Milwaukee, upon arrival at the site of our meeting, we discovered that the emergency brake on the station wagon had failed. I thought it was strange — the automobile wasn't even three months old.

Fortunately, there was a car dealership right behind our motel. The following morning I left it there for repairs. The service manager promised I could pick it up that afternoon. Doris and I decided this was an excellent opportunity for us to do readings. In fact, I had planned to do at least three that day.

She set up the two tape recorders, but just as I was ready to do the reading, one of the tape recorders gave out. We looked at each other as if something mysterious had happened.

Immediately, I looked in the yellow pages for a repair shop. Obviously I was going to have to find one nearby since our car was in the shop all day. But no repair shops were conveniently located, and we felt frustrated. If we were to keep to our tight schedule, we had to get the recorder repaired immediately.

Drawing on my "expert" experience and education as an electronic engineer, I tore into that recorder, bent on repairing it as soon as possible. Well, I couldn't fix it. As a matter of fact, I probably made it worse. Doris and I immediately recognized the humor in the effort and enjoyed a good laugh over my inability to conquer that defective machine. The amusing moment relieved my frustration, and I was able to see the situation in a better perspective. Then it dawned on me. The world, after all, wouldn't come to an end if I got behind in my readings schedule. Doris concurred.

That's when the words again crossed my mind from Psalm 37: "The steps of a good man are ordered by the Lord"—and so are the stops!

I reasoned that God had sent Doris and me a message to slow down. First, the emergency brake on our station wagon failed. He was trying to show us that our physical emergency brake wasn't working—we didn't know when to stop. But when we didn't get that message, God acted again. He stopped the tape recorder so that we couldn't do any more readings.

Reluctantly and obviously disappointed, we packed the recording equipment away and went to the swimming pool and relaxed that entire day. The readings could wait until we got back to Everett.

The last stop on our speaking tour was Livingston, Montana. The meetings were held in our host's home. It was a wonderful time together, and out of those meetings in Livingston we developed the idea for an annual A.I.M. conference. We tentatively planned the first one to be held right there in Livingston about one year hence.

As soon as we arrived home in Everett, the tape recorder was repaired and I started catching up on the scheduled readings. Our lives in Everett were full and rewarding, although Doris and I maintained a hectic and busy schedule. Besides doing the readings, we were traveling here and there for various speaking engagements, keeping the Association running and the newsletter going out. We also had lots of planning to do for that first A.I.M conference.

By now it was clear that we needed secretarial help, and that's when Marlyn joined our work. She and her husband had been active in the Seattle A.R.E. study group and having recently moved to our area, she offered her services. She was like a daughter to Doris and me, and for the next ten years was our devoted friend and colleague.

A year after our first meeting in Montana, we were back for the annual A.I.M. conference. The theme was earth changes, and Livingston was an appropriate location since the earth changes readings mentioned this community prominently as one of the "safe" areas following the upheavals.

Instead of focusing on the physical changes in the earth that might be coming, I urged those attending the conference to look inward, explaining it would be better to think about "internal earthquakes"—necessary inner changes. The earth changes readings explained that if people would begin taking responsibility for their actions and experience a spiritual renewal, the world might be spared the devastation and resulting loss of life and property.

One of the speakers at that conference was Maria DeRungs. She talked about her work, and it was gratifying for me to see someone use the information that I had brought back from the Akashic records in a positive way to help people and relieve their suffering.

For example, she reported on Kali, age two, who had been suffering from a troublesome fear. She had been ill for three weeks and was continually clinging to her mother in this fearful state. After just one session with Wagner's Prelude to Parsifal, she was greatly improved. Both mother and child participated in the music therapy session. The music was played while both were lying down—stomach to stomach—in the attunement

room. A few moments into the session the child relaxed and fell asleep. When she awakened, she was
peaceful and gave the therapist a hug. The next day
her mother reported that Kali was again her happy
self, able to laugh and play.

Over the next five years we sponsored annual A.I.M.
conferences, some held in Livingston and others in
Everett. The conferences were eventually discontinued
because it had become just too much additional work
for us. At the final A.I.M. conference in 1982, a delegation from Japan attended. Unfortunately, none of them
could speak or understand English except Minoru
Kodera, our Japanese contact who was the group's
leader. I was concerned that they would travel all that
distance and not get anything out of the conference;
however, when I expressed this fear to Minoru, he said
not to worry—they wanted to come regardless. I ad-
mired them for their patience. They attended all the
meetings, and as far as I could tell none of them understood a word of what was said.

In 1986 Doris and I grappled over a decision about
the future of A.I.M. For thirteen years we had managed to keep it going with the help of those in our office.
During that time the Association had increased in
membership; however, I no longer had the stamina to
continue with it.

For months Doris and I prayed about this concern,
and although we were reluctant to admit it, the answer was obvious. It was time to discontinue A.I.M.
Time had robbed us of the energy necessary to continue, and rising costs put us in a financial bind. Each
year we would have to take funds from our savings to
meet A.I.M.'s growing expenses. One of the most difficult letters I ever wrote was to members, informing
them that it was necessary to dissolve the Association.

We had to let it go, but still we mourned its passing. The last issue of the A.I.M. quarterly packet was mailed July, 1986.

Age is my adversary, and the passage of time forces me to surrender to my limitations. My reading schedule has now become more flexible, and the number of weekly readings reduced from ten to five. For the past five years Doris and I have kept the last week of each month free to allow us time to catch up, do emergency readings, or take time off to rest.

In the beginning, living in Everett had been so peaceful and quiet. Often Doris and I would drive down to the marina, only five minutes away, and walk along the waters to absorb the energy. We would stroll along the beach, listen to the water lapping up against the shoreline, and think about how satisfying our lives had become following our decision to enter psychic counseling. Life was great for us.

But in the fifteen years we had lived in Everett, it had grown and was no longer the little, quiet town it had been when we moved there. Longtime friends, Dan and Diane, took us for a drive one Sunday afternoon. They wanted us to see the picturesque little town of Anacortes which they had discovered.

We fell in love with it ourselves. We sold our house in Everett, bought a lot overlooking the bay and the distant islands, and built our home there. Since we have lived in our new home since Christmas, 1990, it has been both invigorating and relaxing. We do our work quietly in pleasant surroundings. It seems an appropriate place to spend our senior years.

Looking back we are so thankful to God for His guidance. We have seen "that all things work together for good to them that love God, to them who are the called according to his purpose." (Romans 8:28)

So far, it's been a marvelous journey, this voyage with the spirit. Little would I have realized as a youngster of eighteen making a wartime voyage across the Atlantic that even greater voyages were ahead.

Doris and I have participated in exhilarating educational and enlightening experiences. Some of the lessons we have learned in this life have been easy, fun, and pleasant—others have been difficult, painful, and stressful.

Yet, we know that our life experiences haven't been that much different from anyone else's. Each person has gifts that he or she can use to serve God and other people. Perhaps my gift for psychic counseling seems out of the ordinary and draws attention. But each and every person has talents that we're challenged to use. From meeting those challenges, an individual learns. Certainly, Doris and I have learned from it all, and we are still learning.

Like others, during one period in our lives, we boxed ourselves in very tightly. But little by little we've managed to expand the sides of our box and today breathe more easily. We see a little farther than before. Our area of understanding has broadened, and our capacity for knowledge has deepened. We have gained an appreciation for wisdom and remain convinced that any wisdom we acquired and shared is a result of answered prayers—ours and others'. We are also grateful for our Judeo-Christian foundation—that substructure that opened our eyes to the mysteries of life and girded us for further growth and experiences.

We stand ready to walk through the next door, to soar on wings of spirit toward the next level in our spiritual voyage.

EPILOGUE

As I look back at the extraordinary opportunities given to me by God throughout my life, one theme especially stands out. It's the challenge to go beyond the familiar—to journey past the edge of what's clear and understandable and to go into the unknown. When we come to the edge of all the light we have, seeing nothing but darkness, we must have faith to take that next step.

I began this book with a poem by Claire Norris. I think it's fitting to close with these words again. I hope that the lines of this poem now take on new meaning for you, the reader. Knowing all the changes and spiritual tests I've faced, you will no doubt recognize why this poem is so meaningful to me. I suspect that you'll recognize ways that the poem speaks to the way that God works in your life, too.

When we walk to the edge of all the light we have,
And take the step into the darkness of the unknown,
We must believe one of two things will happen:
There will be something solid
for us to stand on,
or we will be taught how to fly.

APPENDIX

I n more than 22 years of giving life readings, Doris
and I have responded to literally thousands of requests. There is probably no "typical" reading,
although most follow a standard format and style. Here
is one case history presented as an example of our
work.

As you peruse this sample reading, you're sure to
notice that the sentence length and structure isn't always the easiest to understand. Please keep in mind
that I am in a deep meditative state, and from this
altered state of consciousness it isn't easy to communicate in familiar language patterns. But experience
has shown that if people will patiently read and study
what comes through the reading, the meaning is usually evident.

The request for the following life reading came from
Mrs. Ione Jenson, adoptive mother of a nine-year-old
boy. She and her husband, a minister, had adopted
Peter about a year earlier. Peter's natural mother had
abandoned him before he was a year old. He had been
shuffled from home to home for about seven years.
The Jensons heard about him from the boy's natural
grandmother, who happened to be in a prayer group

with Ione and had requested prayer for him several times.

Ione and her husband offered to take Peter into their home if they would be allowed to adopt him. Ione was highly educated in psychology and early childhood education, and the couple seemed very well suited to help Peter. They felt they could give him the home life and love that he sorely needed.

After Peter joined their household, life became quite hectic. He had been on heavy doses of the medication Ritalin for his hyperkinetic behavior, and he didn't sleep well—getting only about three or four hours of sleep most nights. During these sleepless hours, he would often build a fire in his bedroom! Naturally, his new parents didn't get much sleep either!

Ione was in desperate need of some help, and she turned to us for a life reading on Peter. Here, in its entirety, is the transcript of what came.

(Doris) February 8, 1973. This reading is for Peter, age nine, living in . . .

Aron: Goals and challenges to go along with these goals are very important to this soul, for in knowing what goals there are to be attained to, he must also be challenged to attain to these. For having goals without challenges—that is—having goals without any initiative or having been challenged to move on, that can also become frustrating for the inner soul.

Now here we find that inasmuch as this soul has attempted many times to achieve, and he has been very much goal-oriented, yet has he then not necessarily reached to the high place, to that point where he felt he should be, so, therefore, there has been somewhat of a compromise of obtaining his goal and to that

which he has achieved. And each time after achievement so has he not been satisfied, knowing that there
have been other things beyond where he is presently.

So is it also now that goals do mean a great amount
to him, but so do, also, challenges. For presently he is
very much goal-oriented, he has many goals in mind,
so, therefore, the parents, the mother and the father of
him, need likewise to be goal-oriented with him. That
is, they must so construe their lives and so also must
they regulate their lives so as to impart to him the importance of achieving your goals, but not just for the
sheer joy of achieving, but knowing also that the soul
is growing. It is the achievement as well as the goals
obtained, in addition to the other aspects of the universal concepts, namely that of Godliness and
challenge with Godliness—that is—the challenge here
consists in living beyond reproach, living an honest
life, living a life which is full of integrity.

It is here where the individual presently, then known
as you call him, is also situated so he can learn from
those about him, for he has come into this incarnation
particularly so that the parents, that is now his parents, can then help him to achieve, help him to become
more goal-oriented and help him to also achieve the
purposes, not only within the physical, but also within
the spiritual and mental realms.

Presently he has a tremendous intellect and a great
inner desire to venture out into the field of the law.
That is, he desires to be not only a law-abiding citizen,
but he desires also to be a legislator. In other words,
that field within the law itself is what is truly his highest perspective and his highest desire in this present
lifetime.

(Doris: Are you indicating that the study of law would
be good for him?)

Aron: Yes, that's correct.

And so the parents would then have a great opportunity here in helping to formulate ideas, concepts, challenges, goals, with him, for it will be more than just a game. It will be a practice from which the parents themselves will also be able to learn a great amount.

Now, his Life Seal is then that type of a Life Seal which truly is not seen very often; but in this case, so has it been with him for many a lifetime, and he has attempted to achieve to this particular goal, as we see it here. Now his Life Seal is namely that of an open—a wide open—rose. And directly in the center there is a gold ring. This seal is not seen very often simply because most people are quite secretive about their inner desires, but here is a person who is rather open with that which he has. He is free to share and willing to share.

But he also demands somewhat from those who are around him, particularly at the age in which he is now. But after about five to seven years, much of the demands will be then taken away and be substituted for a goal-oriented life, if the parents then can institute that within him and can instill that goal-orientation within him.

We also find that directly above the rose with the gold ring, there is here a precious stone, or a gemstone, which is that of a pearl. This is a pearl from India, which as he grows in maturity, it would be well for him to have just a single pearl on a chain. Then that chain could be worn either in his clothing such as a necktie, that is, around the necktie like a neckchain—necktie chain—or it could be worn even, or used in his own pocket as a keychain with a pearl on the one end.

Now the pearl would be a very welcome sign for him, for as he then would touch the pearl, so will there be some very warm and very concise vibrations emanating from the pearl which would help him greatly in his meditations—to hold the pearl in his left hand and capping it, or cupping his right hand over the pearl would then also help to stimulate his own desire and his own interest within not only the religious field, the spiritual atmosphere and environment, but also within the field whereby his talents are lying, namely within that of law, that of the legal field, even to the point of him becoming a legislator and an administrator.

Now surrounding the rose with the circle in it, the gold circle, and the pearl above it, there is here a six-pointed figure. This six-pointed figure is now in the color of lavender.

(Doris: You're not talking about a star, are you?)

Aron: No, no, no. Not a star. It is a six-pointed figure such as a - a figure with six sides on it.

(Doris: All right, sort of like a square, only it has six sides.)

Aron: Six sides on it, that's correct. And these six sides, now, represent his many facets. For example, the top side represents his impatience. The side on the right, going now in a clockwise direction, depicts also his desire for accuracy. The third side shows his desire to be known and also to be accepted. The fourth side shows his ingenuity when things seemingly go wrong, then he can modify many a thing. The fifth side is that of his heart toward God. And the sixth side is also his openness with all people. In other words, many times he can get himself in trouble by being too open, but then, he will share freely with those who are willing to hear him. It would be well for the parents to understand this very aspect, for it is, then, good that they would instill within him some discernment and some discretion, wisdom is that what he needs. For, then, even Christ did not commit Himself to all people, for He knew what was in all men. All right then.

(Doris: Would you give a brief summary of the influences which have been affecting Peter in this life?)

Aron: The strongest influence within him is that from Neptune, followed by Mercury. Neptune and Mercury together form, then, a triangle with Mars. Mars is giving the activity, Mercury the direction, and Nepture the power. It is in this direction that he is now oriented for he has the desire, but he is not truly goal-oriented. He is scattering many of his energies in many directions and thus he is dissipating himself to his own detriment.

He also finds it difficult to keep his interest up after he has started on many interesting and even thought-provoking tasks. So, therefore, it is up to the parents to reduce the scope of his tasks so that he does not take on too much and then lose interest, but that they will keep up the interest by encouraging him, and by assessing from time to time what it is that he has accomplished — even to the point of writing these achievements down on a little book that he can keep for himself and thus be able to see the progress which he has made from one step to another. This is very important for him, for he, as we said, desires to do all things very accurately, but he also needs the direction required so he can achieve to the point where he needs to be so he can continue on with his law practice and with the study and the training to be the legislator which he also has the talent and the heart for.

He is not out in this life to gain much fame for himself. He is out here to help mankind. And the best way he can help mankind is namely through the law of

legislation as well as being a person who, then, re-
spects both law and order. He is a very orderly person
himself, but then, he has tendencies to over-react and
be so orderly that it can almost kill him. And with this
we shall go on.

(Doris: Would you discuss now the predominant past
lives that have been influencing Peter in this life?)

Aron: At the height of the development in Atlantis,
so were you here with your present brother. You were
brothers. And at this time, though your brother was in
the field of science, yet you had, then, gone into the
field of law, being at this time an attorney. And you
had many marvelous and wonderful achievements,
but you were never satisfied with your achievements,
and you were always looking for that which lay beyond
your immediate results, your immediate success. You
had become so accustomed to achievement that you
have taken them for granted, and if you would ever
lose any cases, or any case, or if you did not obtain
that which you think you should have obtained, you
became rather despondent.

You were running, here, a life on a very high amount
of nervous—but also emotional—energy, and you were
always looking to find the goose with the golden egg. In
other words, you were looking for shortstops, and you
were also looking for shortcuts. In other words, here,
you were looking for that which would take you to the
result, to the goal immediately. And this was not always achievable, but, nevertheless, you did have so
many marvelous successes. And here you began the
search, not very seriously, but casually, so to speak,
into the religious life. You did not attend too many of
the services, or even listen to much of the religion
which was taught and also propagated at that time in
Atlantis.

But for the most part, you kept within your activities. You did not make fun nor think lowly of those who were very well entuned within the field of religion. But you respected them. But you would not have much to do with it yourself, simply because you did not think it was very practical. For here you were a man of material means. You were a man of material wealth. And so, in this present lifetime, there has to be a different association, a different orientation within yourself so that you will begin to think not only of the material but also of the spiritual and mental faculties, and integrate all these into unity with your God.

After that lifetime, so were you at the Great Pyramid — during the building of the Great Pyramid. You were, then, a negotiator for material. In other words, you would be traveling from place to place to find the stones, the huge stones - and then having them brought down by some very complex, but yet simple means — simple devices — and placed, then, directly into the pyramid. Even the way the stones were cut were then accomplished by having some very sharp beams of light at a very high frequency. And one could cut with that very quickly and measure off any type of a length one desired. And thus, also elevate this stone with anti-gravity measures, and thus be able to place any type of stone even while it was being elevated, cutting it to size right at the site, right at the spot, and then slowly and meticulously fitting it in. And then the weather, the sand, which was then poured in between the spots, or the spaces between the stones — the sand together with the rain and the weather would then cement it in over the years as it has been there.

You negotiated quite strongly and also you had some very strong terms that you demanded much from those who obtained for you the stones, and you were never satisfied with what you obtained. Though you did an excellent job, yet did you judge yourself too harshly. You were too hard on yourself. And the end result of this was that you suffered greatly within the physical body. You began to suffer within your legs, both the left and the right leg, and also in the hip and in the upper part of your spine. And these are the four spots to watch for in your present lifetime. It is suggested that you take some Vitamin B, some Vitamin D, and some Vitamin A. E, also, is necessary from time to time.

It is likewise here, that you had eye trouble and that you had difficulties in seeing, particularly at night. And here again, it is because you overdid yourself. You were too difficult on yourself and you were never satisfied with yourself. You hardly treated yourself as a human being. And this again is a typical trait which you have carrying over with you. So this is one thing that you should watch over, for you in this lifetime—simply to treat yourself kindly, but also to accept yourself where you are as you grow into maturity on the physical level.

Now, after that lifetime, you were then, at the time of Christ, in Palestine. Here you were then achieving and attaining to become an attorney. But you never did, you were frustrated, and you tried many times. And you then had to resort to just becoming a scribe. And this never set well with you because you felt you were below your calling. And you could never relegate—or even could never accept—the position which you had to take simply because you did not have the means, the funds to obtain the training to become a lawyer. And neither did you have the influence. You went in with an attitude—that of a bull in a china closet—but you mellowed rather quickly when you realized that you did not have the wherewithal—that is, the means to become a lawyer, to become an attorney. And you also saw this becoming an attorney was much of a social club, a social gathering where everybody would agree with one another, and there was very little of independent thinking.

Now, when Christ came on the scene, so did you then immediately accept Him, and for this you were cast out from your position. And you again became very frustrated for here you had hoped that you would rise to become an attorney. But now when you were cast out from your position, so did you have nothing else you could do but either to follow Christ, or to become a fisherman. And you became the latter, a fisherman. And here again, you felt that you were below your dignity, and so you had rather a difficult time physically in Palestine. But spiritually, it was well worth it for you gained much here, though your attitudes could have been much better. They would have helped you greatly had you so had a much more hopeful and a happier attitude in living with yourself.

After that lifetime, so were you in China in the 5th century A.D. where you were here with your present parents. And here you became a pottery maker, a person who was teaching pottery, even to the point where you could teach pottery as a hobby in your present lifetime. And this also would be an excellent medium for you to generate much of the creative energies, but also to dissipate some of your other desires which you now have in so many directions.

China also has an influence upon you that if you should ever happen to obtain a small Chinese figure carved in ivory and placed next to your bed, so would that be also a very welcome and helpful sign for you. For that ivory figure will help you then to regain again that status which you had in China, namely that of confidence. For you knew then that you could work very diligently with your hands and thus produce.

Now, after that lifetime, so were you then in Spain, this time in about the 1300s, where here you were then rather a wealthy man within your own means, owning land. You even had many people working for you. Thus you had two working for you who now are also in your family—your father and your present brother. And these were working with books within your own private collection. And you treated them very kindly, you treated all of your people rather kindly. And it is for this reason that you also have a tendency in this lifetime to treat all men the same, and you can also aspire, you have the talent to again regain wealth. But keep in mind that though your motives in Spain were not necessarily of the highest, yet by changing your motives and desiring that which would help mankind, so can you again regain that wealth; but also this time on a higher plane with the spiritual factors so situated that they will help you to grow more than you could ever hope to realize.

After that lifetime, you were in the 1800s in that place which is then called Fort Dearborn, and later it became the place where Chicago is built. And it is here that you were then again starting to become a lawyer, starting to become an attorney. But inasmuch as you did not have any opportunities, you did not have anyone to help you, so did you have to give that up, and you became, instead, a metalsmith—like a blacksmith working diligently with the metals and doing good work, but not being very happy about it.

You see, you have had many opportunities given to you, not that which you necessarily have wanted to do, but that which has been necessary for your own growth. And though you have done good work, your attitudes have not been that which would have helped you even more. For it is not so much WHAT you do, but it is with what attitudes you perform your task. Your name, first name (and middle name) was Thomas, your middle name was Michael. All right then. Yes, your parents were here with you in the 1800s, the same as you have now. All right.

(Doris: His present parents?)

Aron: Yes, that's correct.

(Doris: What colors are influencing his spiritual centers at this time?)

Aron: His spiritual centers presently are now influenced by the red, is influencing the Gonad Center. The Cells of Leydig is being influenced by emerald green. The Adrenal Center is being influenced by orange. Here where there is some great activities and also some agitation on the inner man, there is turmoil. And yet that orange is needed simply because it will give him strength and courage. But for the next two to three years, so do we suggest that he also find some pink in his surroundings. This would be very, very helpful for him. It will quiet him down, together with lavender, and not only on the outside, but more on the inside. It is not so much for the outside circumstances.

Now, the Thymus is influenced by a very bright yellow. He has great intellect. And the Thyroid is influenced by a very light blue. He desires to do things, but he does not have any particular goals. So therefore, his mind, to make it up, is not yet present. He does not have the presence of mind to make decisions and to stick by them. In other words, convictions are not his easiest path. So we suggest that he be then clothed presently in some darker blue, such as a royal or a medium blue, or anything in that shade. And then later on to teach him some color meditations such that he can visualize the colors going from the lighter to the darker blue (for the Thyroid color), and thus be able to make up his mind to even a stronger degree—but not that he is to be strong-willed, or even to the point of becoming hard-headed, but rather, flexible.

Now, the Pineal is influenced by lavender. And the Pituitary, by purple. Now, this lavender is the color that he came in on. Though he came in with a very ambitious program, with the right tutoring and with the right guidance, he should be able to achieve his goals. And this is the reason why he chose the parents, that they should be his parents, that he would have an opportunity to achieve to his long-, long-considered dream, namely, to again enter into the field of law. That he could be of help to many people—with the right attitudes and the right perspectives. All right.

(Doris: He was sent to these parents for that reason?)

Aron: That's correct. That's correct. So you see, these parents also have a responsibility, for as they are helping him, he also, in turn, in the future will be of tremendous help to them in more ways than one. All right.

(Doris: What is his main purpose, then, for coming into this life?)

Aron: He came in to be a legislator, a lawyer, a teacher within the realms of the spirit; to bring about, within the law, also the law of God. To bring about within the legislation and the administration of many activities, the concept that God is overall, and it is from Him that all knowledge and wisdom must come. In other words, he would be a forerunner into a new form, a new type of legislation whereby government will then be in sessions not so much to rule the people, nor to subjugate the people, but to help develop the people into the beings that they should be. All right.

(Doris: What would you suggest that he do, and that

his parents might help him to do, to make sure he accomplishes this?)

Aron: Here then, encourage him. Also help him to set goals and help him to accomplish these goals. As you pray with him, also make him realize that in every little bit, in every little way that he is living, that this also is counting for his accomplishment; no matter how small, no matter how large. It is, then, the matter of being faithful to that which he is doing.

To read about—particularly Abraham Lincoln, which is one of his favorite books, by the way; and to read also about George Washington, Thomas Jefferson, and many of the early fathers of the country where you are presently living, would be rather helpful for him. It is well also that he should read of—that is, when he grows older—about men like Origen and Augustine; to read also about the ancient lawyers in both Rome and Greece, and about the French philosophers—would come in later on. In the meantime, keep him encouraged with the things which are at hand. Keep him also realizing that he is a being greatly loved of God, and that he IS important to the entire universe, and that his contribution will count as to the betterment of mankind.

Keep him, also, in tune with his God, such as with the fellowship and with the knowledge of his Christ, the Christ that is the Redeemer, not the consciousness, nor a principle, but a person. Keep him also realizing that as he does to others, so will others likewise also do to him—in other words—as you sow, you reap. Teach him as well—to love himself as well as others. And above all things, to love his God.

There is much that the parents can do in encouraging him in setting practical goals for him and having him, then, follow these up and checking up on him. In other words, to outline a program for him that he can carry forth in accordance with the desires of his own impulses and his own initiative and intuition.

It is important that all of the family members come together at least once a week for, then, a family council, that they can share one with another, what has taken place, what is going wrong, what is going right, what the progress is, and what else can be done in order to encourage one another. Allow it to be a time of cooperation. Cooperation is a two-way street, not a one-way street. Cooperation means that two or more must cooperate, one with another in order to fulfill the central goals. And presently, the central goals now are the unity and the prosperity and the fulfillment in life, and the abundant life of the entire family.

Wrapped in that which we have mentioned, this also—the purposes and goals of this soul to which we have been speaking, (and it is very important that he also realizes) that to love his God with all that he is, with all that he has, and with all that he can be, is equally as important as to prepare for his studies within the field of law. And with this, we are finished.

(Doris: All right. Thank you very much.)

Ione and her husband applied the information from this reading very wisely. To surround Peter in lavender and pink, she bought lavender sheets for his bed and made him a pair of pink pajamas. "After the second night of sleeping in these colors," she wrote us, "he slept for twelve straight hours." They were able to withdraw him from all medication. He loved those pajamas, and wouldn't give them up until he was fourteen years old. The pajama pants hit him just below the knee, by that time.

Some years later, Ione attended a seminar in Baltimore, given by a psychiatrist. During his lecture he had touched on the subject of hyperkinetic behavior in children. Afterward, she shared with him about her experience with pink pajamas and lavender sheets. Excitedly, he told her that lavender is the color of light that comes through the womb, and pink is the vibration of mother-love. He confided that he had several hyperkinetic behavioral patients. He would be eager to suggest those colors for them.

In a recent letter to us about Peter's reading, Ione brought us up to date. Dressing him in dark blue was easy, since blue jeans were the common standard of dress. "To this day," she wrote, "blue is his preferred color." When as an adult Peter heard his reading for the first time, he chuckled and said, "Mom, isn't it interesting that I joined the navy out of high school and wore navy blue for five years!"

Ione went on to say that shortly after they adopted Peter, her husband remarked that every time she left for a few days—or even a few hours—that Peter tried to take control of the household and order both him and their older son around. Both she and her husband had laughed when the reading found the three fellows sharing a lifetime in Spain, where both her husband and older son were Peter's servants.

Ione and her husband followed the reading's suggestion to set goals and keep a journal of the progress made. They gathered their family once a week to discuss how well each one (Ione and her husband, as well) were succeeding in accomplishing their goals. This had worked very well, and Peter hadn't felt singled out as the only one needing to change his attitudes and behavior.

As yet, Peter hasn't become an attorney, but Ione

has observed that he has always had a "very legally oriented mind." Instead he graduated in May, 1992, with a bachelor's degree in computer science. She wrote that the high degree of intelligence reported in the reading was very accurate. As the reading suggested, he has also been a joy to them in his adult years.

What Is A.R.E.?

The Association for Research and Enlightenment, Inc. (A.R.E.®), is the international headquarters for the work of Edgar Cayce (1877-1945), who is considered the best-documented psychic of the twentieth century. Founded in 1931, the A.R.E. consists of a community of people from all walks of life and spiritual traditions, who have found meaningful and life-transformative insights from the readings of Edgar Cayce.

Although A.R.E. headquarters is located in Virginia Beach, Virginia—where visitors are always welcome—the A.R.E. community is a global network of individuals who offer conferences, educational activities, and fellowship around the world. People of every age are invited to participate in programs that focus on such topics as holistic health, dreams, reincarnation, ESP, the power of the mind, meditation, and personal spirituality.

In addition to study groups and various activities, the A.R.E. offers membership benefits and services, a bimonthly magazine, a newsletter, extracts from the Cayce readings, conferences, international tours, a massage school curriculum, an impressive volunteer network, a retreat-type camp for children and adults, and A.R.E. contacts around the world. A.R.E. also maintains an affiliation with Atlantic University, which offers a master's degree program in Transpersonal Studies.

For additional information about A.R.E. activities hosted near you, please contact:

A.R.E.
67th St. and Atlantic Ave.
P.O. Box 595
Virginia Beach, VA 23451-0595
(804) 428-3588

A.R.E. Press

A.R.E. Press is a publisher and distributor of books, audiotapes, and videos that offer guidance for a more fulfilling life. Our products are based on, or are compatible with, the concepts in the psychic readings of Edgar Cayce.

We especially seek to create products which carry forward the inspirational story of individuals who have made practical application of the Cayce legacy.

For a free catalog, please write to A.R.E. Press at the address below or call toll free 1-800-723-1112. For any other information, please call 804-428-3588.

**A.R.E. Press
Sixty-Eighth & Atlantic Avenue
P.O. Box 656
Virginia Beach, VA 23451-0656**